The Pleasure of
POETRY

Also by Kingsley Amis

KINGSLEY AMIS

The Pleasure of
POETRY

FROM HIS DAILY MIRROR COLUMN

CASSELL

Cassell Publishers Limited
Villiers House, 41/47 Strand
London WC2N 5JE, England

Introduction © Kingsley Amis 1990
Selection and Commentary © The Daily Mirror 1986

First published 1990

British Library Cataloguing in Publication Data
The pleasure of poetry: from his *Daily
Mirror* column.
1. Poetry in English – Anthologies
I. Amis, Kingsley, *1922*–
821.008

ISBN 0-304-31907-4

Typeset in Linotron Joanna by Litho Link Ltd, Welshpool, Powys, Wales
Printed and bound in Great Britain by Mackays of Chatham Ltd

Contents

Poem Titles

MARCH

JUNE

SEPTEMBER

DECEMBER

Introduction

When my friend Mike Molloy, editor of the *Daily Mirror*, said to me at a drinks party, 'How would you like to be our poetry editor?' I thought he was joking or, at most, expressing an idle fancy. But it happened, in its way the most remarkable event in the world of poetry since the last war. A popular newspaper started to print, five times a week, a poem, a serious poem, a poem selected from the 600-year tradition of English poetry.

Molloy had long suspected that, at a time when most 'modern poetry' is meaningless or too private to be understood and seldom deigns to rhyme or scan, there is still a big potential audience for what most people see as traditional or real or proper poetry that tells a story, describes a scene, creates or evokes a mood or an emotion, and does all these things and more in terms that the ordinary educated reader can understand, embrace and appreciate, now and then acquiring in this way something that might enhance the rest of his or her life. This kind of poetry usually rhymes and scans, thus making it easier to remember as well as more pleasant to the normal ear. Now all these are quite familiar sentiments. The significant point was that Mike Molloy could test them in practice. So the *Daily Mirror* Poetry Column began.

Well, that potential audience turned out to be there all right. We had thought that perhaps the response would emerge largely from the older age-groups, from those who had come across the poems at school, or poems like them. Such people did approve heartily, but we were greatly cheered by the number of younger people who showed that the capacity to respond to poetry in the old sense does not weaken when most contemporary 'poetry' gets written largely in the new sense — or non-sense. Dozens of letters showed that it was not necessary to have been taught about Blake or Wordsworth or Anne Brontë or Housman, or even to have heard of them before, in order to appreciate them. We noticed too, and rejoiced, that poetry that was modern by date but possible to understand and appreciate had no prejudice against it: what the readers disliked was not the dates (say) 1930–1980, but meandering absurdity.

My part in all this, apart from sharing in the general enthusiasm, was to choose the daily poem, do a bit of quiet surgery if needed on the hard or antiquated words, even a small cut now and again, and write a short paragraph explaining the poem, introducing the poet, etc. I also had to provide for a certain amount of day-to-day variety. All this turned out to be the most enjoyable job I ever had, but it was not the easiest. It still irks me that I had to pass over so much fine stuff that was too antique, obscure in its reference or setting, or simply too long or too short to fit the necessarily severe limits set me. But I found out a lot I ought to have known before – you never go into what a poem *really* means until you have to, and you never have to until you have to explain it to a general, not a specialised, audience. My explanation of Gray's Elegy may be wrong, but at least it answers several questions nobody had thought of asking before.

I did a little bit of extra research out of curiosity, such as asking the BBC what poems were most often asked for on their verse request programmes (the favourite one of all, I was fascinated to discover, was Leigh Hunt's 'Abou Ben Adhem') and it reinforced the conclusion Molloy and I had originally had and found confirmed, that there are two poetry publics in this country, one small and greatly over-exposed, the other large and desperately short of the material, the books, it craves for. (Libraries are often no help.) This volume will, it is hoped, please and encourage the second of these two publics. (I personally think the first is on the decline, but that may just be wishful thinking.)

On the morning when the first *Mirror* poem came out – 'Remember', number 50 in this book – the Features Editor of the paper telephoned to say he has just had a call from a woman telling him she had never heard of Christina Rossetti before, but on reading the poem had gone straight out and bought the author's collected works. Perhaps it wasn't much, but it seemed to me in itself to make the whole enterprise worth while, and it reinforced the pleasure and the pride I had felt on being called upon to undertake the task of editorship.

Kingsley Amis

The Golden Journey to Samarkand

JAMES ELROY FLECKER

We who with songs beguile your pilgrimage
And swear that Beauty lives though lilies die,
We Poets of the proud old lineage
Who sing to find your hearts, we know not why, –

What shall we tell you? Tales, marvellous tales
Of ships and stars and isles where good men rest,
Where nevermore the rose of sunset pales,
And winds and shadows fall toward the West:

And there the world's first huge white-bearded kings
In dim glades sleeping, murmur in their sleep,
And closer round their breasts the ivy clings,
Cutting its pathway slow and red and deep.

And how beguile you? Death has no repose
Warmer and deeper than that Orient sand
Which hides the beauty and bright faith of those
Who made the Golden Journey to Samarkand.

And now they wait and whiten peaceably,
Those conquerors, those poets, those so fair:
They know time comes, not only you and I,
But the whole world shall whiten, here or there;

When those long caravans that cross the plain
With dauntless feet and sound of silver bells
Put forth no more for glory or for gain,
Take no more solace from the palm-girt wells.

When the great markets by the sea shut fast
All that calm Sunday that goes on and on:
When even lovers find their peace at last,
And Earth is but a star, that once had shone.

Flecker spent some years as a consular official in Beirut and other parts of the
Middle East, and was familiar with the languages and literatures of the region.
Here he sees himself as a teller of tales on the caravan route to Samarkand,
once a centre of Arab culture, now in the USSR. Flecker died of tuberculosis in
Switzerland at the age of thirty.

Paradise

JOHN MILTON

His fair large front and eye sublime declared
    Absolute rule; and hyacinthine locks
Round from his parted forelock manly hung
    Clustering, but not beneath his shoulders broad:
She as a veil down to the slender waist
    Her unadorned golden tresses wore
Dishevelled, but in wanton ringlets waved
    As the vine curls her tendrils, which implied
Subjection, but required with gentle sway,
    And by her yielded, by him best received,
Yielded with coy submission, modest pride,
    And sweet reluctant amorous delay.
Nor those mysterious parts were then concealed,
    Then was not guilty shame, dishonest shame,
Of nature's works, honour dishonourable,
    Sin-bred, how have ye troubled all mankind
With shows instead, mere shows of seeming pure,
    And banished from man's life his happiest life,
Simplicity and spotless innocence.
    So passed they naked on, nor shunned the sight
Of God or angel, for they thought no ill:
    So hand in hand they passed, the loveliest pair
That ever since in love's embraces met,
    Adam the goodliest man of men since born
His sons, the fairest of her daughters Eve.
    Under a tuft of shade that on a green
Stood whispering soft, by a fresh fountain side
    They sat them down . . .
About them frisking played
    All beasts of the earth, since wild, and of all chase
In wood or wilderness, forest or den;
    Sporting the lion ramped, and in his paw
Dandled the kid; bears, tigers, ounces, pards,
    Gambolled before them, the unwieldy elephant
To make them mirth used all his might, and wreathed
    His lithe proboscis; close the serpent sly
Insinuating, wove with Gordian twine
    His braided train, and of his fatal guile
Gave proof unheeded; others on the grass
    Couched, and now filled with pasture gazing sat,

> Or bedward ruminating: for the sun
>> Declined was hasting now with prone career
> To the Ocean Isles, and in the ascending scale
>> Of heaven the stars that usher evening rose.

*This extract from Paradise Lost shows us Paradise itself, with Adam and Eve
in the Garden of Eden. To write this scene took all Milton's skill, tact and
courage, especially the candid description of the pair in their nakedness, at a
time when puritanism was so powerful. Adam's 'large front' is his broad
forehead; an ounce is a snow-leopard.*

Bagpipe Music   3

LOUIS MACNEICE

It's no go the merry-go-round, it's no go the rickshaw,
    All we want is a limousine and a ticket for the peepshow.
Their knickers are made of crêpe-de-chine, their shoes are made of python,
    Their halls are lined with tiger rugs and their walls with heads of bison.

John MacDonald found a corpse, put it under the sofa,
    Waited till it came to life and hit it with a poker,
Sold its eyes for souvenirs, sold its blood for whisky,
    Kept its bones for dumb-bells to use when he was fifty.

It's no go the Yogi-Man, it's no go Blavatsky,
All we want is a bank balance and a bit of skirt in a taxi.

Annie MacDougall went to milk, caught her foot in the heather,
    Woke to hear a dance record playing of Old Vienna,
It's no go your maidenheads, it's no go your culture,
    All we want is a Dunlop tyre and the devil mend the puncture.

The Laird o' Phelps spent Hogmanay declaring he was sober,
    Counted his feet to prove the fact and found he had one foot over.
Mrs Carmichael had her fifth, looked at the job with repulsion.
    Said to the midwife 'Take it away; I'm through with over-production'.

It's no go the gossip column, it's no go the ceilidh,
All we want is a mother's help and a sugar-stick for the baby.

[continued]

Willie Murray cut his thumb, couldn't count the damage,
    Took the hide of an Ayrshire cow and used it for a bandage.
His brother caught three hundred cran when the seas were lavish,
    Threw the bleeders back in the sea and went upon the parish.

It's no go the Herring Board, it's no go the Bible,
All we want is a packet of fags when our hands are idle.

It's no go the picture palace, it's no go the stadium,
    It's no go the country cot with a pot of pink geraniums,
It's no go the Government grants, it's no go the elections,
    Sit on your arse for fifty years and hang your hat on a pension.

It's no go my honey love, it's no go my poppet;
    Work your hands from day to day, the winds will blow the profit,
The glass is falling hour by hour, the glass will fall for ever,
    But if you break the bloody glass you won't hold up the weather.

*Of all the poets who appeared in the 1930s MacNeice (born in Belfast) was the
liveliest and the most spontaneous, qualities that can be seen in this poem
which has become something of a classic. It could be called nonsense verse, but
it becomes a fairly bleak commentary on the frivolity of modern life, a sad one
too at the end.*

4   *Ode to the North-East Wind*

CHARLES KINGSLEY

Welcome, wild North-easter,
    Shame it is to see
Odes to every zephyr,
    Ne'er a verse to thee.

Welcome, black North-easter!
    O'er the German foam;
O'er the Danish moorlands
    From thy frozen home.

. . . . . .

Sweep the golden reed-beds;
    Crisp the lazy dyke;
Hunger into madness
    Every plunging pike.

Fill the lake with wild-fowl
  Fill the marsh with snipe;
While on dreary moorlands
  Lonely curlew pipe.

Through the black fir-forest
  Thunder harsh and dry,
Shattering down the snow-flakes
  Off the curdled sky.

      .   .   .   .   .   .

Let the luscious South-wind
  Breathe in lovers' sighs,
While the lazy gallants
  Bask in ladies' eyes.

What does he but soften
  Heart alike and pen?
'Tis the hard grey weather
  Breeds hardy English men.

      .   .   .   .   .   .

But the black North-easter,
  Through the snowstorm hurled,
Drives our English hearts of oak
  Seaward round the world.

Come, as came our fathers,
  Heralded by thee,
Conquering from the eastward,
  Lords by land and sea.

Come; and strong within us
  Stir the Viking's blood;
Bracing brain and sinew,
  Blow, thou wind of God!

In his lifetime Kingsley was named the proponent of 'muscular Christianity',
all hearty optimism, beer and cricket. That side of him certainly comes
out here. I am not, I think, at all his kind of person, but I simply cannot
help being carried away by this poem (even in this abbreviated version).
A zephyr is a mild breeze.

5

Upon Kinde and True Love

AURELIAN TOWNSHEND

'Tis not how witty, nor how free,
Nor yet how beautiful she be,
But how much kinde and true to me.
Freedom and Wit none can confine,
And Beauty like the Sun doth shine,
But kinde and true are onely mine.

Let others with attention sit,
To listen, and admire her wit,
That is a rock where I'le not split.
Let others dote upon her eyes,
And burn their hearts for sacrifice,
Beauty's a calm where danger lyes.

But Kinde and True have been long tried
A harbour where we may confide,
And safely there at anchor ride.
From change of winds there we are free,
And need not feare Storme's tyrannie,
Nor Pirat, though a Prince he be.

Townshend was a courtier, steward to the powerful Robert Cecil, close friend of
Ben Jonson and writer of entertainments for Charles I. He is supposed to have
disappeared during the Civil War. This lyric of his strikes an unusual note. To
be 'free' in this sense was to be spontaneous, lively. Confide – feel confident.

The Toys

COVENTRY PATMORE

My little Son, who look'd from thoughtful eyes
And moved and spoke in quiet grown-up-wise,
Having my law the seventh time disobey'd,
I struck him, and dismiss'd
With hard words and unkiss'd,
– His mother, who was patient, being dead.
Then, fearing lest his grief should hinder sleep,
I visited his bed,
But found him slumbering deep,
With darken'd eyelids, and their lashes yet
From his late sobbing wet.
And I, with moan,
Kissing away his tears, left others of my own;
For, on a table drawn beside his head,
He had put, within his reach,
A box of counters and a red vein'd stone,
A piece of glass abraded by the beach,
And six or seven shells,
A bottle with bluebells,
And two French copper coins, ranged there with careful art,
To comfort his sad heart.
So when that night I pray'd
To God, I wept, and said:
Ah! When at last we lie with trancèd breath,
Not vexing Thee in death,
And Thou rememberest of what toys
We made our joys,
How weakly understood
Thy great commanded good,
Then, fatherly not less
Than I whom Thou hast moulded from the clay,
Thou'lt leave Thy wrath, and say,
'I will be sorry for their childishness.'

---

*Unusually for a Victorian, Coventry Kersey Dighton Patmore wrote a number
of poems about commonplace domestic life. As this one suggests, his wife died
before her time. He was a deeply religious man who was converted to Roman
Catholicism in middle age. For many years he was an assistant at what is now
the British Library.*

A Psalm of Life

HENRY WADSWORTH LONGFELLOW

Tell me not, in mournful numbers,
    'Life is but an empty dream!'
For the soul is dead that slumbers,
    And things are not what they seem.

Life is real! Life is earnest!
    And the grave is not its goal;
'Dust thou art, to dust returnest!',
    Was not spoken of the soul.

Not enjoyment, and not sorrow,
    Is our destined end or way;
But to act, that each to-morrow
    Find us farther than to-day.

Art is long, and Time is fleeting,
    And our hearts, though stout and brave,
Still, like muffled drums, are beating –
    Funeral marches to the grave.

In the world's broad field of battle,
    In the bivouac of Life,
Be not like dumb, driven cattle!
    Be a hero in the strife!

Trust no Future, howe'er pleasant!
    Let the dead Past bury its dead!
Act – act in the living Present!
    Heart within, and God o'erhead!

Lives of great men all remind us
    We can make our lives sublime,
And, departing, leave behind us
    Footprints on the sands of time;

Footprints, that perhaps another,
    Sailing o'er life's solemn main,
A forlorn and shipwrecked brother,
    Seeing, shall take heart again.

Let us, then, be up and doing,
    With a heart for any fate;
Still achieving, still pursuing,
    Learn to labor and to wait.

*Longfellow was born in Maine and become a professor at Harvard. He wrote
many well-known poems, including 'Excelsior' and the longish Hiawatha.
This one is vigorous enough in its rather breezy, optimistic way, but those
footprints have always bothered me a little. Footprints even in damp sand tend
not to last long.*

The Nightjar   8

SIR HENRY NEWBOLT

We loved our Nightjar, but she would not stay with us.
We had found her lying as dead, but soft and warm,
Under the apple tree beside the old thatched wall.
Two days we kept her in a basket near the fire,
Fed her, and thought she well might live – till suddenly
In the very moment of most confiding hope
She raised herself all tense, quivered and drooped and died.
Tears sprang into my eyes – why not? the heart of man
Soon sets itself to love a living companion,
The more so if by chance it asks some care of him.
And this one had the kind of loveliness that goes
Far deeper than the optic nerve – full fathom five
To the soul's ocean cave, where Wonder and Reason
Tell their alternate dreams of how the world was made.
So wonderful she was – her wings the wings of night
But powdered here and there with tiny golden clouds
And wave-line markings like sea-ripples on the sand.
    O how I wish I might forget that bird –
        Never!
    – But even now, like all beauty of earth,
She is fading from me into the dusk of Time.

*Newbolt is usually remembered for his patriotic poems – such as 'Drake's
Drum' and 'Vitaï Lampada' (no. 22), but he had a tender, almost feminine,
side to him, as seen in this little poem. It reads like the record of a real
experience with a seeming naturalness that is a tribute to his skill.*

9

In My Own Shire

A. E. HOUSMAN

In my own shire, if I was sad,
Homely comforters I had:
The earth, because my heart was sore,
Sorrowed for the son she bore;
And standing hills, long to remain,
Shared their short-lived comrade's pain.
And bound for the same bourn as I,
On every road I wandered by
Trod beside me, close and dear,
The beautiful and death-struck year:
Whether in the woodland brown
I heard the beechnut rustle down,
And saw the purple crocus pale
Flower about the autumn dale;
Or littering far the fields of May
Lady-smocks a-bleaching lay,
And like a skylit water stood
The bluebells in the azured wood.

Yonder, lightening other loads,
The seasons range the country roads,
But here in London streets I ken
No such helpmates, only men;
And these are not in plight to bear,
If they would, another's care.
They have enough as 'tis: I see
In many an eye that measures me
The mortal sickness of a mind
Too unhappy to be kind.
Undone with misery, all they can
Is to hate their fellow man;
And till they drop they needs must still
Look at you and wish you ill.

Housman was not a rural sort of person in his life, but no English poet has
described the countryside better than or more lovingly than he. The feeling that
one is a kind of exile in a town, like the character in this poem, is quite
common among people who would never dream of living anywhere else.
A lady-smock (properly, 'lady's-smock') is a pale pink meadow flower.

Elegy in a Country Churchyard 10

THOMAS GRAY

The curfew tolls the knell of parting day,
The lowing herd wind slowly o'er the lea,
The ploughman homeward plods his weary way,
And leaves the world to darkness and to me.

Now fades the glimmering landscape on the sight,
And all the air a solemn stillness holds,
Save where the beetle wheels his droning flight,
And drowsy tinklings lull the distant folds.

Save that from yonder ivy-mantled tow'r
The moping owl does to the moon complain
Of such as, wandering near her secret bow'r,
Molest her ancient solitary reign.

Beneath those rugged elms, that yew-tree's shade,
Where heaves the turf in many a mould'ring heap,
Each in his narrow cell for ever laid,
The rude forefathers of the hamlet sleep.

The breezy call of incense-breathing morn,
The swallow twitt'ring from the straw-built shed,
The cock's shrill clarion or the echoing horn,
No more shall rouse them from their lowly bed.

For them no more the blazing hearth shall burn,
Or busy housewife ply her evening care:
No children run to lisp their sire's return,
Or climb his knees the envied kiss to share.

Oft did the harvest to their sickle yield,
Their furrow oft the stubborn glebe has broke;
How jocund did they drive their team afield!
How bow'd the woods beneath their sturdy stroke!

Let not Ambition mock their useful toil,
Their homely joys and destiny obscure;
Nor Grandeur hear, with a disdainful smile,
The short and simple annals of the poor.

The boast of heraldry, the pomp of pow'r,
And all that beauty, all that wealth e'er gave,
Awaits alike th'inevitable hour.
The paths of glory lead but to the grave.

[continued]

Nor you, ye Proud, impute to these the fault,
If Mem'ry o'er their tomb no trophies raise,
Where thro' the long-drawn aisle and fretted vault
The pealing anthem swells the note of praise.

Can storied urn or animated bust
Back to its mansion call the fleeting breath?
Can Honour's voice provoke the silent dust,
Or Flatt'ry sooth the dull cold ear of Death?

Perhaps in this neglected spot is laid
Some heart once pregnant with celestial fire;
Hands, that the rod of empire might have sway'd,
Or wak'd to extasy the living lyre.

But Knowledge to their eyes her ample page
Rich with the spoils of time did ne'er unroll:
Chill Penury repress'd their noble rage,
And froze the genial current of the soul.

Full many a gem of purest ray serene.
The dark unfathom'd caves of ocean bear:
Full many a flower is born to blush unseen,
And waste its sweetness on the desert air.

Some village-Hampden, that with dauntless breast
The little Tyrant of his fields withstood;
Some mute inglorious Milton here may rest,
Some Cromwell guiltless of his country's blood.

Th'applause of list'ning senates to command,
The threats of pain and ruin to despise,
To scatter plenty o'er a smiling land,
And read their hist'ry in a nation's eyes,

Their lot forbade: nor circumscrib'd alone
Their growing virtues, but their crimes confin'd;
Forbade to wade through slaughter to a throne,
And shut the gates of mercy on mankind.

The struggling pangs of conscious truth to hide,
To quench the blushes of ingenuous shame,
Or heap the shrine of Luxury and Pride
With incense kindled at the Muse's flame.

Far from the madding crowd's ignoble strife,
Their sober wishes never learn'd to stray;
Along the cool sequester'd vale of life
They kept the noiseless tenor of their way.

Yet ev'n these bones from insult to protect
Some frail memorial still erected nigh,
With uncouth rhymes and shapeless sculpture deck'd,
Implores the passing tribute of a sigh.

Their name, their years spelt by th'unletter'd muse,
The place of fame and elegy supply:
And many a holy text around she strews,
That teach the rustic moralist to die.

For who to dumb Forgetfulness a prey,
This pleasing anxious being e'er resign'd,
Left the warm precincts of the cheerful day,
Nor cast one longing lingering look behind?

On some fond breast the parting soul relies,
Some pious drops the closing eye requires:
Ev'n from the tomb the voice of Nature cries,
Ev'n in our ashes live their wonted fires.

For thee who, mindful of the unhonour'd dead,
Dost in these lines their artless tale relate;
If chance, by lonely Contemplation led,
Some kindred spirit shall inquire thy fate.

Haply some hoary-headed swain may say,
'Oft have we seen him at the peep of dawn
Brushing with hasty steps the dews away
To meet the sun upon the upland lawn.

'There at the foot of yonder nodding beech
That wreathes its old fantastic roots so high,
His listless length at noontide would he stretch,
And pore upon the brook that babbles by.

'Hard by yon wood, now smiling as in scorn,
Mutt'ring his wayward fancies he would rove,
Now drooping, woeful wan, like one forlorn,
Or craz'd with care, or cross'd in hopeless love.

'One morn I miss'd him on the custom'd hill,
Along the heath and near his fav'rite tree;
Another came; nor yet beside the rill,
Nor up the lawn, nor at the wood was he;

'The next with dirges due in sad array
Slow through the church-way path we saw him borne.
Approach and read (for thou can'st read) the lay,
Grav'd on the stone beneath yon aged thorn.

[continued]

'(There scatter'd oft, the earliest of the Year,
By hands unseen, are show'rs of violets found;
The red-breast loves to build and warble there,
And little footsteps lightly print the ground.)'

THE EPITAPH

Here rests his head upon the lap of earth
A youth to Fortune and to Fame unknown.
Fair Science frowned not on his humble birth,
And Melancholy mark'd him for her own.

Large was his bounty and his soul sincere,
Heav'n did a recompense as largely send:
He gave to mis'ry all he had, a tear,
He gained from Heav'n ('twas all he wished) a friend.

No farther seek his merits to disclose.
Or draw his frailties from their dread abode,
(There they alike in trembling hope repose)
The bosom of his Father and his God.

Gray was a Cambridge professor who often visited the village of Stoke Poges in
Buckinghamshire, the churchyard of which is supposed to have inspired this
famous Elegy, though recent research points rather to nearby Burnham
Beeches. The success of the Elegy led to his being offered the laureateship, which
he declined. 'Thee' in verse 24 must refer to Gray himself, who appears in the
verses following not as he was, but as he imagines he would have been if
– instead of being born in London and going to Eton and Cambridge –
he had been a villager: illiterate, unable to use his poetic gift and reduced to
'muttering his wayward fancies' to himself, finally dying before his time of
frustration and despair.

The Garden of Proserpine 11

ALGERNON CHARLES SWINBURNE

Here, where the world is quiet;
    Here, where all trouble seems
Dead winds' and spent waves' riot
    In doubtful dreams of dreams;
I watch the green field growing
For reaping folk and sowing,
For harvest-time and mowing,
    A sleepy world of streams.

I am tired of tears and laughter,
    And men that laugh and weep;
Of what may come hereafter
    For men that sow to reap:
I am weary of days and hours,
Bloom buds of barren flowers,
Desires and dreams and powers
    And everything but sleep.

. . . .

We are not sure of sorrow,
    And joy was never sure;
To-day will die to-morrow;
    Time stops to no man's lure;
And love, grown faint and fretful,
With lips but half regretful
Sighs, and with eyes forgetful
    Weeps that no loves endure.

From too much love of living,
    From hope and fear set free,
We thank with brief thanks-giving
    Whatever gods may be
That no life lives for ever;
That dead men rise up never;
That even the weariest river
    Winds somewhere safe to sea.

[continued]

Then star nor sun shall waken,
Nor any change of light;
Nor sound of waters shaken,
Nor any sound or sight:
Nor wintery leaves nor vernal,
Nor days nor things diurnal;
Only the sleep eternal
In an eternal night.

Algernon Charles Swinburne, friend of Rossetti and his circle, was like many men of his time, an enthusiastic republican and anti-clerical. A writer of great buoyancy, he manages here to make death and oblivion positively attractive. Proserpine is the Roman goddess of the infernal regions and also of sleep.

12

Tommy

RUDYARD KIPLING

I went into a public-'ouse to get a pint o' beer,
The publican 'e up an' sez, 'We serve no red-coats here.'
The girls be'ind the bar they laughed an' giggled fit to die,
I outs into the street again, an' to myself sez I:

O it's Tommy this, an' Tommy that, an' 'Tommy, go away';
But it's 'Thank you, Mister Atkins,' when the band begins to play –
The band begins to play, my boys, the band begins to play,
O it's 'Thank you, Mister Atkins,' when the band begins to play.

I went into a theatre as sober as could be,
They gave a drunk civilian room, but 'adn't none for me;
They sent me to the gallery or round the music-'alls,
But when it comes to fightin', Lord! they'll shove me in the stalls!

For it's Tommy this, an' Tommy that, an' 'Tommy, wait outside';
But it's 'Special train for Atkins' when the trooper's on the tide –
The troopship's on the tide, my boys, the troopship's on the tide,
O it's 'Special train for Atkins' when the trooper's on the tide.

Yes, makin' mock o' uniforms that guard you while you sleep
Is cheaper than them uniforms, an' they're starvation cheap;
An' hustlin' drunken soldiers when they're going large a bit
Is five times better business than paradin' in full kit.

Then it's Tommy this, an' Tommy that, an' 'Tommy, ow's yer soul?'
But it's 'Thin red line of 'eroes' when the drums begin to roll –
The drums begin to roll, my boys, the drums begin to roll,
O it's 'Thin red line of 'eroes' when the drums begin to roll.

We aren't no thin red 'eroes, nor we aren't no blackguards too,
But single men in barricks, most remarkable like you;
An' if sometimes our conduck isn't all your fancy paints,
Why, single men in barricks don't grow into plaster saints;

While it's Tommy this, an' Tommy that, an' 'Tommy fall be'ind',
But it's 'Please to walk in front, sir,' when there's trouble in the wind –
There's trouble in the wind, my boys, there's trouble in the wind,
O it's 'Please to walk in front, sir,' when there's trouble in the wind,

You talk o' better food for us, an' schools, an' fires, an' all:
We'll wait for extry rations if you treat us rational.
Don't mess about the cook-room slops, but prove it to our face
The Widow's Uniform is not the soldier-man's disgrace.

For it's Tommy this, an' Tommy that, an' 'Chuck him out, the brute!'
But it's 'Saviour of 'is country' when the guns begin to shoot;
An' it's Tommy this, an' Tommy that, an' anything you please;
An' Tommy ain't a bloomin' fool – you bet that Tommy sees!

Johnny

13

W. H. AUDEN

O the valley in the summer where I and my John
Beside the deep river would walk on and on
While the flowers at our feet and the birds up above
Argued so sweetly on reciprocal love,
And I leaned on his shoulder; 'O Johnny, let's play':
But he frowned like thunder and he went away.

O that Friday near Christmas as I well recall
When we went to the Charity Matinee Ball,
The floor was so smooth and the band was so loud
And Johnny so handsome I felt so proud;
'Squeeze me tighter, dear Johnny, let's dance till it's day':
But he frowned like thunder and he went away.

[continued]

Shall I ever forget at the Grand Opera
When music poured out of each wonderful star?
Diamonds and pearls they hung dazzling down
Over each silver or golden silk gown;
'O John I'm in heaven,' I whispered to say:
But he frowned like thunder and he went away.

O but he was as fair as garden in flower,
As slender and tall as the great Eiffel Tower,
When the waltz throbbed out on the long promenade
O his eyes and his smile they went straight to my heart;
'O marry me, Johnny, I'll love and obey':
But he frowned like thunder and he went away.

O last night I dreamed of you, Johnny, my lover,
You'd the sun on one arm and the moon on the other,
The sea it was blue and the grass it was green,
Every star rattled a round tambourine;
Ten thousand miles deep in a pit there I lay:
But you frowned like thunder and you went away.

*This is one of four cabaret songs that Auden wrote for the singer Hedli
Anderson, wife of his friend Louis MacNeice. If the original intention was to
produce a light, frothy piece then something went wrong, for most readers will
find this a genuinely touching poem, made more so by the deliberate banality of
some of the phrases.*

from
Beppo

GEORGE GORDON, LORD BYRON

With all its sinful doings, I must say,
    That Italy's a pleasant place to me,
Who love to see the Sun shine every day,
    And vines (not nail'd to walls) from tree to tree
Festoon'd, much like the back scene of a play,
    Or melodrame, which people flock to see,
When the first act is ended by a dance
In vineyards copied from the south of France.

. . . .

I love the language, that soft bastard Latin,
  Which melts like kisses from a female mouth,
And sounds as if it should be writ on satin,
  With syllables which breathe of the sweet South,
And gentle liquids gliding also pat in,
  That not a single accent seems uncouth,
Like our harsh northern whistling, gruntling guttural,
Which we're obliged to hiss, and spit, and sputter all.

· · · · · · ·

'England! with all thy faults I love thee still',
  I said at Calais, and have not forgot it;
I like to speak and lucubrate my fill;
  I like the government (but that is not it);
I like the freedom of the press and quill;
  I like the Habeas Corpus (when we've got it);
I like a Parliamentary debate
Particularly when tis' not too late;

I like the taxes, when they're not too many;
  I like a seacoal fire, when not too dear;
I like a beef-steak, too, as well as any;
  Have no objection to a pot of beer;
I like the weather – when it is not rainy,
  That is, I like two months of every year.
And so God save the Regent, Church, and King!
Which means that I like all and everything.

Our standing army, and disbanded seamen,
  Poor's rate, Reform, my own, the nation's debt,
Our little riots just to show we're free men,
  Our trifling bankruptcies in the Gazette,
Our cloudy climate, and our chilly women,
  All these I can forgive, and those forget,
And greatly venerate our recent glories,
And wish they were not owing to the Tories.

Byron was everything that could possibly be meant by a romantic poet but he
was also one of the best writers of light verse, entertaining, technically brilliant,
full of personal asides. Beppo appeared in 1818; its more ambitious successor,
Don Juan, was never finished. If it had been it might have outshone all
Byron's other works.

The Soldier's Dream

15

THOMAS CAMPBELL

Our bugles sang truce, for the night-cloud had lower'd,
　　And the sentinel stars set their match in the sky;
And thousands had sunk on the ground overpower'd,
　　The weary to sleep, and the wounded to die.

When reposing that night on my pallet of straw
　　By the wolf-scaring faggot that guarded the slain,
At the dead of the night a sweet Vision I saw;
　　And thrice ere the morning I dreamt it again.

Methought from the battle-field's dreadful array
　　Far, far I had roam'd on a desolate track:
'Twas Autumn – and sunshine arose on the way
　　To the home of my fathers, that welcom'd me back.

I flew to the pleasant fields travers'd so oft
　　In life's morning march, when my bosom was young;
I heard my own mountain-goats bleating aloft,
　　And knew the sweet strain that the corn-reapers sung.

Then pledged we the wine-cup, and fondly I swore
　　From my home and my weeping friends never to part;
My little ones kiss'd me a thousand times o'er,
　　And my wife sobb'd aloud in her fullness of heart.

'Stay – stay with us – rest! – thou art weary and worn!' –
　　And fain was their war-broken soldier to stay; –
But some sorrow return'd with the dawning of morn,
　　And the voice in my dreaming ear melted away.

*Campbell was born in Glasgow and soon began a poetical career. In 1800 he
visited Germany, finding himself in Regensburg near Munich just before it was
captured by invading French forces. He took shelter in a Scottish monastery.
This experience of war on his doorstep no doubt suggested to him poems like
this one.*

The Sparrows' Chorus

ELIZABETH JENNINGS

How often you forget about us! We are
About all through the year.
Our feathers are drab, beside other birds we appear
Nonentities, no fashion parades for us.
Nobody makes a fuss
Of us and really we don't care,
At least, not too much.
But we are faithful, whatever the weather we stay
Among you. And don't think we're ungrateful for the food
Some of you like to toss.
We need it badly. We can lose half of our weight
On an icy night. We depend a lot on you.

Often, we have to admit, we wish we wore
Flamboyant colours. A yellow, a red, a blue.
The robin is lucky and all the tits are too.
But perhaps our smallness is noticeable. Beside
A starling or blackbird we are almost invisible
But don't forget we are here,
Domestic creatures, never flying far.
Just to exist through an English climate is
Remarkable.
It's almost a miracle simply that we are.

*Elizabeth Jennings has written on some deeply personal matters like childhood,
love and religion. Another of her subjects is animals, not an easy one because
of the danger of becoming arch or twee. She never is. Here she makes
us pay attention to some very ordinary, unspectacular creatures we mostly
take for granted.*

Last Lines

EMILY BRONTË

No coward soul is mine,
No trembler in the world's storm-troubled sphere;
I see Heaven's glories shine,
And faith shines equal, arming me from fear.

O God within my breast,
Almighty, ever-present Deity!
Life – that in me has rest,
As I, undying Life, have power in Thee!

Vain are the thousand creeds
That move men's hearts, unutterably vain;
Worthless as withered weeds,
Or idlest froth amid the boundless main,

To waken doubt in one
Holding so fast by Thine infinity;
So surely anchored on
The steadfast rock of immortality.

With wide-embracing love
Thy spirit animates eternal years,
Pervades and broods above,
Changes, sustains, dissolves, creates, and rears.

Though earth and man were gone,
And suns and universes ceased to be,
And Thou were left alone,
Every existence would exist in Thee.

There is not room for Death,
Nor atom that his might could render void:
Thou – Thou art Being and Breath,
And what Thou art may never be destroyed.

Emily Brontë is probably best remembered today for her novel Wuthering
Heights, but some of her poems are often considered finer. This one shows her
undaunted by the sufferings and sorrows of her short life. Her toughness was
such that she refused to have a doctor called until two hours before her death
from tuberculosis.

from
The Lay of the Last Minstrel 18

SIR WALTER SCOTT

Breathes there the man, with soul so dead,
Who never to himself hath said,
   This is my own, my native land!
Whose heart hath ne'er within him burn'd,
As home his footsteps he hath turn'd,
   From wandering on a foreign strand!
If such there breathe, go, mark him well;
For him no Minstrel raptures swell;
High though his titles, proud his name,
Boundless his wealth as wise can claim;
Despite those titles, power, and pelf,
The wretch, concentred all in self,
Living, shall forfeit fair renown,
And, doubly dying, shall go down
To the vile dust, from whence he sprung,
Unwept, unhonoured, and unsung.

O Caledonia! stern and wild,
Meet nurse for a poetic child!
Land of brown heath and shaggy wood,
Land of the mountain and the flood,
Land of my sires! what mortal hand
Can e'er untie the filial band,
That knits me to thy rugged strand!
Still, as I view each well-known scene,
Think what is now, and what hath been,
Seems as, to me, of all bereft,
Sole friends thy woods and streams were left;
And thus I love them better still,
Even in extremity of ill.
By Yarrow's stream still let me stray,
Though none should guide my feeble way;
Still feel the breeze down Ettrick break,
Although it chill my wither'd cheek;
Still lay my head by Teviot Stone,
Though there, forgotten and alone,
The Bard may draw his parting groan.

*Scott, a man of colossal energy, was a busy Edinburgh lawyer who found time
to write a great deal of poetry and many novels. His main subject was Scotland
and Scottish history, something new in those days when even Scotch whisky
was virtually unheard of south of the Border. The first half of this extract was
once a favourite recitation piece. (Caledonia is Scotland.)*

19 Light Breaks Where No Sun Shines

DYLAN THOMAS

Light breaks where no sun shines;
Where no sea runs, the waters of the heart
Push in their tides;
And, broken ghosts with glow-worms in their heads,
The things of light
File through the flesh where no flesh decks the bones.

A candle in the thighs
Warms youth and seed and burns the seeds of age;
Where no seed stirs,
The fruit of man unwrinkles in the stars,
Bright as a fig;
Where no wax is, the candle shows its hairs.

Dawn breaks behind the eyes;
From poles of skull and toe the windy blood
Slides like a sea;
Nor fenced, nor staked, the gushers of the sky
Spout to the rod
Divining in a smile the oil of tears.

Night in the sockets rounds,
Like some pitch moon, the limit of the globes;
Day lights the bone;
Where no cold is, the skinning gales unpin
The winter's robes;
The film of spring is hanging from the lids.

Light breaks on secret lots,
On tips of thought where thoughts smell in the rain;
When logics die,
The secret of the soil grows through the eye,
And blood jumps in the sun;
Above the waste allotments the dawn halts.

In almost everything Thomas wrote he created a particular kind of excitement no one else has matched, what seems a quite new sense that the realms of the imagination are infinite, and if he sometimes seems to deliver less than he promises, the excitement is real enough. He must have attracted hundreds of thousands of people to poetry.

Come into the Garden, Maud   20

ALFRED, LORD TENNYSON

Come into the garden, Maud,
  For the black bat, night, has flown,
Come into the garden, Maud,
  I am here at the gate alone;
And the woodbine spices are wafted abroad,
  And the musk of the rose is blown.

For a breeze of morning moves,
  And the planet of Love is on high,
Beginning to faint in the light that she loves
  On a bed of daffodil sky,
To faint in the light of the sun she loves,
  To faint in his light, and to die.

All night have the roses heard
  The flute, violin, bassoon;
All night has the casement jessamine stirr'd
  To the dancers dancing in tune;
Till a silence fell with the waking bird,
  And a hush with the setting moon.

      .   .   .   .

Queen rose of the rosebud garden of girls,
  Come hither, the dances are done,
In gloss of satin and glimmer of pearls,
  Queen lily and rose in one;
Shine out, little head, sunning over with curls,
  To the flowers, and be their sun.

There has fallen a splendid tear
  From the passion-flower at the gate.
She is coming, my dove, my dear;
  She is coming, my life, my fate;
The red rose cries, 'She is near, she is near;'
  And the white rose weeps, 'She is late;'
The larkspur listens, 'I hear, I hear;'
  And the lily whispers, 'I wait'.

[continued]

She is coming, my own, my sweet;
Were it ever so airy a tread,
My heart would hear her and beat,
Were it earth in an earthy bed;
My dust would hear her and beat,
Had I lain for a century dead;
Would start and tremble under her feet,
And blossom in purple and red.

The long poem Maud is a kind of monologue or verse novel in the first person. The story is fiction and yet full of recognisable bits of Tennyson's life. The song (printed here in a shortened version) closes Part I with an outpouring of the ecstasy and exultation of young love. Understandably, it has been set to music many times.

21

from
The Prelude

WILLIAM WORDSWORTH

And in the frosty season, when the sun
Was set, and visible for many a mile
The cottage windows through the twilight blaz'd,
I heeded not the summons: – happy time
It was, indeed, for all of us; to me
It was a time of rapture: clear and loud
The village clock toll'd six; I wheel'd about,
Proud and exulting, like an untir'd horse,
That cares not for his home. – All shod with steel,
We hiss'd along the polish'd ice, in games
Confederate, imitative of the chace
And woodland pleasures, the resounding horn,
The pack loud bellowing, and the hunted hare,
So through the darkness and the cold we flew,
And not a voice was idle; with the din,
Meanwhile, the precipices rang aloud,
The leafless trees, and every icy crag
Tinkled like iron, while the distant hills
Into the tumult sent an alien sound
Of melancholy, not unnoticed, while the stars,
Eastward, were sparkling clear, and in the west
The orange sky of evening died away.
Not seldom from the uproar I retired

Into a silent bay, or sportively
Glanced sideways, leaving the tumultuous throng,
To cut across the image of a star
That gleam'd upon the ice: and oftentimes
When we had given our bodies to the wind,
And all the shadowy banks, on either side,
Came sweeping through the darkness, spinning still
The rapid line of motion; then at once
Have I, reclining back upon my heels,
Stopp'd short, yet still the solitary cliffs
Wheeled by me, even as if the earth had roll'd
With visible motion her diurnal round;
Behind me did they stretch in solemn train
Feebler and feebler, and I stood and watch'd
Till all was tranquil as a dreamless sleep.

The Prelude is a long autobiographical poem in fourteen books about the poet's youth. His recollections or recreations of his childhood and schooldays are extraordinarily vivid. Wordsworth had special feelings about childhood, believing it to be a time when human beings are closer to God than in their corrupt adult life.

Vitaï Lampada   22

SIR HENRY NEWBOLT

There's a breathless hush in the Close to-night –
   Ten to make and the match to win –
A bumping pitch and a blinding light,
   An hour to play and the last man in.
And it's not for the sake of a ribboned coat,
   Or the selfish hope of a season's fame,
But his Captain's hand on his shoulder smote –
   'Play up! play up! and play the game!'

The sand of the desert is sodden red, –
   Red with the wreck of a square that broke; –
The Gatling's jammed and the Colonel dead,
   And the regiment blind with dust and smoke.

[continued]

The river of death has brimmed his banks,
    And England's far, and Honour a name,
But the voice of a schoolboy rallies the ranks:
    'Play up! play up! and play the game!'

This is the word that year by year,
    While in her place the School is set,
Every one of her sons must hear,
    And none that hears it dare forget.
This they all with a joyful mind
    Bear through life like a torch in flame,
And falling fling to the host behind –
    'Play up! play up! and play the game!'

*The title means the Torch of Life, flaming like the Olympic torch. Newbolt is
writing here about unselfishness, the team spirit and tradition rather than war
as such. His approach to the matter is unfashionable now, but there are still
some people who will understand it.*

23   # The Howling of Wolves

TED HUGHES

Is without world.

What are they dragging up and out on their long leashes of sound

That dissolve in the mid-air silence?

Then crying of a baby, in this forest of starving silences,
Brings the wolves running.
Tuning of a violin, in this forest delicate as an owl's ear,
Brings the wolves running – brings the steel traps clashing and slavering,
The steel furred to keep it from cracking in the cold,
The eyes that never learn how it has come about
That they must live like this,

That they must live

Innocence crept into minerals.

The wind sweeps through and the hunched wolf shivers.
It howls you cannot say whether out of agony or joy.

The earth is under its tongue,
A dead weight of darkness, trying to see through its eyes.
The wolf is living for the earth.
But the wolf is small, it comprehends little.

It goes to and fro, trailing its haunches and whimpering horribly.

It must feed its fur.

The night snows stars and the earth creaks.

This characteristic poem shows Hughes exploring an aspect of animal life, not just describing from the outside as a traditional nature poet might have done but trying as well to get under the skin of the subject. Although his style is distinctive and individual his work is not hard to follow.

When My Love Swears That She Is Made of Truth

24

WILLIAM SHAKESPEARE

When my love swears that she is made of truth,
I do believe her, though I know she lies;
That she might think me some untutor'd youth,
Unlearned in the world's false subtleties.
Thus vainly thinking that she thinks me young,
Although she knows my days are past the best,
Simply I credit her false-speaking tongue:
On both sides thus is simple truth supprest.
But wherefore says she not she is unjust?
And wherefore say not I that I am old?
O, love's best habit is in seeming trust,
And age in love loves not to have years told:
    Therefore I lie with her; and she with me,
    And in our faults by lies we flatter'd be.

This sonnet is one of the series addressed to the so-called Dark Lady, meaning dark-haired – the Elizabethans generally preferred blondes, at any rate in their writings. Shakespeare is in down-to-earth mood here; the pun in line 13 is characteristic. He was not much over forty when he wrote the sonnets, but that was quite old in those days.

25

Come Back to Erin

CHARLOTTE ALINGTON BARNARD

Come back to Erin, Mavourneen, Mavourneen!
    Come back, Aroon, to the land of thy birth,
Come with the shamrocks and springtime, Mavourneen,
    And it's Killarney shall ring with our mirth.
Sure, when we lent ye to beautiful England,
    Little we thought of the lone winter days,
Little we thought of the hush of the starshine
    Over the mountain, the bluffs, and the braes!
Then come back to Erin, Mavourneen, Mavourneen!
Come back again to the land of thy birth!
    Come back to Erin, Mavourneen, Mavourneen!
And it's Killarney shall ring with our mirth.

Over the green sea, Mavourneen, Mavourneen,
    Long shone the white sail that bore thee away,
Riding the white waves that fair summer mornin',
    Just like a May-flow'r afloat on the bay.
O but my heart sank when clouds came between us,
    Like a grey curtain the rain falling down,
Hid from my sad eyes the path o'er the ocean,
    Far, far away where my colleen had flown.

O may the angels awakin' and sleepin'
    Watch o'er my bird in the land far away!
And it's my pray'rs will consign to their keepin'
    Care o' my jewel by night and by day.
When by the fireside I watch the bright embers,
    Then all my heart flies to England and thee,
Cravin' to know if my darlin' remembers,
    Or if her thoughts may be crossin' to me.

This is a typical mid-Victorian ballad, designed for singing and still popular in
living memory. Some modern readers are likely to find it sentimental; others
will see charm in it, even if it is a period charm. Mavourneen means my
darling, and maybe I should add that Erin is the ancient poetic name for
Ireland.

from
The Deserted Village

OLIVER GOLDSMITH

Ill fares the land, to hastening ills a prey,
Where wealth accumulates and men decay:
Princes and lords may flourish or may fade;
A breath can make them, as a breath has made;
But a bold peasantry, their country's pride,
When once destroyed, can never be supplied.

A time there was, ere England's griefs began,
When every rood of ground maintained its man;
For him light labour spread her wholesome store,
Just gave what life required, but gave no more:
His best companions, innocence and health;
And his best riches, ignorance of wealth.

But times are altered; trade's unfeeling train
Usurp the land and dispossess the swain;
Along the lawn, where scattered hamlets rose,
Unwieldy wealth and cumbrous pomp repose;
And every want to opulence allied,
And every pang that folly pays to pride.
These gentle hours that plenty bade to bloom,
Those calm desires that asked but little room,
Those healthful sports that graced the peaceful scene,
Lived in each look and brightened all the green;
These, far departing, seek a kinder shore,
And rural mirth and manners are no more.

. . . .

Sweet was the sound, when oft at evening's close
Up yonder hill the village murmur rose;
There, as I passed with careless steps and slow,
The mingling notes came softened from below;
The swain responsive as the milkmaid sung,
The sober herd that lowed to meet their young;
The noisy geese that gabbled o'er the pool,
The playful children just let loose from school;
The watchdog's voice that bayed the whispering wind,
And the loud laugh that spoke the vacant mind;
These all in sweet confusion sought the shade,
And filled each pause the nightingale had made.

[continued]

But now the sounds of population fail,
No cheerful murmurs fluctuate in the gale,
No busy steps the grassgrown foot-way tread,
For all the bloomy flush of life is fled.

*Goldsmith's subject in his long poem is a very real one, the depopulation of the
countryside in the later eighteenth century. He spent four or five years travelling
round and collecting material and also drew on memories of his boyhood in
Ireland. The village in the poem is a composite, intended to be typical.*

27

Love

GEORGE HERBERT

Love bade me welcome; yet my soul drew back;
    Guilty of dust and sin.
But quick-ey'd Love, observing me grow slack
    From my first entrance in,
Drew nearer to me, sweetly questioning,
    If I lack'd any thing.

'A guest,' I answer'd, 'worthy to be here':
    Love said, 'You shall be he.'
'I the unkind, ungrateful? Ah, my dear,
    I cannot look on Thee.'
Love took my hand, and smiling did reply,
    'Who made the eyes but I?'

'Truth, Lord; but I have marr'd them; let my shame
    Go where it doth deserve.'
'And know you not,' says Love, 'Who bore the blame?'
    'My dear, then I will serve.'
'You must sit down,' says Love, 'and taste My meat.'
    So I did sit and eat.

*Like the other Metaphysical poets, Herbert was given to far-fetched images and
strange comparisons. Here, he casts Our Lord (divine Love) as an innkeeper
offering refreshment to a weary traveller. He puts such feeling into the dialogue
between the two that the result is never merely ingenious. The religious
symbolism is clear and straightforward.*

The Moon and the Yew Tree   28

SYLVIA PLATH

This is the light of the mind, cold and planetary.
The trees of the mind are black. The light is blue.
The grasses unload their griefs on my feet as if I were God,
Prickling my ankles and murmuring their humility.
Fumey, spiritous mists inhabit this place
Separated from my house by a row of headstones.
I simply cannot see where there is to get to.

The moon is no door. It is a face in its own right,
White as a knuckle and terribly upset.
It drags the sea after it like a dark crime; it is quiet
With the O-gape of complete despair. I live here.
Twice on Sunday, the bells startle the sky –
Eight great tongues affirming the Resurrection.
At the end, they soberly bong out their names.

The yew tree points up. It has a Gothic shape.
The eyes lift after it and find the moon.
The moon is my mother. She is not sweet like Mary.
Her blue garments unloose small bats and owls.
How I would like to believe in tenderness –
The face of the effigy, gentled by candles,
Bending, on me in particular, its mild eyes.

I have fallen a long way. Clouds are flowering
Blue and mystical over the face of the stars.
Inside the church, the saints will be all blue,
Floating on their delicate feet over the cold pews,
Their hands and faces stiff with holiness.
The moon sees nothing of this. She is bald and wild.
And the message of the yew tree is blackness – blackness and silence.

*Sylvia Plath, an American, found and kept a following among readers of poetry,
largely because of the intensely personal voice in everything she wrote. Some
have found it too personal, even self-centred, and her subject is never anything
but herself. But there is no doubt about her originality and curious power.*

29 # Fear of Death

JOHN ASHBERY

What is it now with me
And is it as I have become?
Is there no slate free from the boundary lines
Of before and after? The window is open today

And the air pours in with piano notes
In its skirts, as though to say, 'Look, John,
I've brought these and these' – that is,
A few Beethovens, some Brahmses,

A few choice Poulenc notes. . . . Yes,
It is being free again, the air, it has to keep coming back
Because that's all it's good for.
I want to stay with it out of fear

That keeps me from walking up certain steps,
Knocking at certain doors, fear of growing old
Alone, and of finding no one at the evening end
Of the path except another myself

Nodding a curt greeting: 'Well, you've been awhile
But now we're back together, which is what counts.'
Air in my path, you could shorten this,
But the breeze has dropped, and silence is the last word.

Ashbery has a great following in his native America, where he has more than once been called the greatest poet now writing in the English language. British readers have been more cautious. His meaning is usually implied rather than stated and it is sometimes hard to gain more than a general impression.

That Day

RUDYARD KIPLING

It got beyond all orders an' it got beyond all 'ope;
　　It got to shammin' wounded an' retirin' from the 'alt.
'Ole companies was lookin' for the nearest road to slope;
　　It were just a bloomin' knock-out – an' our fault!

　　　Now there ain't no chorus 'ere to give,
　　　　Nor there ain't no band to play;
　　　An' I wish I was dead 'fore I done what I did,
　　　　Or seen what I seed that day!

　　　　　.　.　.　.　.　.　.

There was thirty dead an' wounded on the ground we wouldn't keep –
　　No, there wasn't more than twenty when the front begun to go –
But, Christ! along the line o' flight they cut us up like sheep,
　　An' that was all we gained by doin' so!

I 'eard the knives be'ind me, but I dursn't face my man,
　　Nor I don't know where I went to, 'cause I didn't 'alt to see,
Till I 'eard a beggar squealin' out for quarter as 'e ran,
　　An' I thought I knew the voice an' – it was me!

We was 'idin' under bedsteads more than 'arf a march away:
　　We was lyin' up like rabbits all about the country-side;
An' the Major cursed 'is Maker 'cause 'e'd lived to see that day,
　　An' the Colonel broke 'is sword acrost, an' cried.

We was rotten 'fore we started – we was never disciplined;
　　We made it out a favour if an order was obeyed.
Yes, every little drummer 'ad 'is rights an' wrongs to mind,
　　So we had to pay for teachin' – an' we paid!

The papers 'id it 'andsome, but you know the Army knows:
　　We was put to groomin' camels till the regiments withdrew,
An' they gave us each a medal for subduin' England's foes,
　　An' I 'ope you like my song – because it's true!

　　　An' there ain't no chorus 'ere to give,
　　　　Nor there ain't no band to play;
　　　But I wish I was dead 'fore I done what I did,
　　　　Or seen what I seed that day!

Kipling was indeed the poet of Empire, but he had no illusions about the
practical results on the people who managed it and kept it together.
Although he never served in the army he knew perfectly well that during
a battle everybody is terrified and that there are times when even British
troops run away.

In a Notebook

JAMES FENTON

There was a river overhung with trees
With wooden houses built along its shallows
From which the morning sun drew up a haze
And the gyrations of the early swallows
Paid no attention to the gentle breeze
Which spoke discreetly from the weeping willows.
There was a jetty by the forest clearing
Where a small boat was tugging at its mooring.

And night still lingered underneath the eaves.
In the dark houseboats families were stirring
And Chinese soup was cooked on charcoal stoves.
Then one by one there came into the clearing
Mothers and daughters bowed beneath their sheaves.
The silent children gathered round me staring
And the shy soldiers setting out for battle
Asked for a cigarette and laughed a little.

From low canoes old men laid out their nets
While on the bank young boys with lines were fishing.
The wicker traps were drawn up by their floats.
The girls stood waist-deep in the river washing
Or tossed the day's rice on enamel plates
And I sat drinking bitter coffee wishing
The tide would turn to bring me to my senses
After the pleasant war and the evasive answers.

There was a river overhung with trees.
The girls stood waist-deep in the river washing,
And night still lingered underneath the eaves
While on the bank young boys with lines were fishing.
Mothers and daughters bowed beneath their sheaves
While I sat drinking bitter coffee wishing –
And the tide turned and brought me to my senses.
The pleasant war brought the unpleasant answers.

The villages are burnt, the cities void;
The morning light has left the river view;
The distant followers have been dismayed;
And I'm afraid, reading this passage now,

That everything I knew has been destroyed
By those whom I admired but never knew;
The laughing soldiers fought to their defeat
And I'm afraid most of my friends are dead.

Fenton's high repute as the best poet of his generation derives in part from his unusual flair for the technical side of verse-writing. He has travelled widely and has developed great powers of description. Here he refers to his experiences as a freelance correspondent in Vietnam and Cambodia.

Coming

32

PHILIP LARKIN

On longer evenings,
Light, chill and yellow,
Bathes the serene
Foreheads of houses.
A thrush sings,
Laurel-surrounded
In the deep bare garden,
Its fresh-peeled voice
Astonishing the brickwork.
It will be spring soon,
It will be spring soon –
And I, whose childhood
Is a forgotten boredom,
Feel like a child
Who comes on a scene
Of adult reconciling,
And can understand nothing
But the unusual laughter,
And starts to be happy.

Larkin has said that, as far as he is concerned, a successful poem takes an experience – something seen or felt or imagined – and puts it into words in such a way as to preserve it, to hand it on to the reader. Few experiences can have be handed on more clearly, concisely and memorably than this moment in late winter.

The Dream of Gerontius
from

33

JOHN HENRY NEWMAN

Praise to the Holiest in the height,
 And in the depth be praise,
In all His works most wonderful;
 Most sure in all His ways!

O loving wisdom of our God!
 When all was sin and shame,
A second Adam to the fight
 And to the rescue came.

O wisest love! that flesh and blood,
 Which did in Adam fail,
Should strive afresh against the foe,
 Should strive and should prevail;

And that a higher gift than grace
 Should flesh and blood refine,
God's presence and His very Self,
 And Essence all-divine.

O generous love! that He who smote
 In man for man the foe,
The double agony in man
 For man should undergo;

And in the garden secretly
 And on the cross on high,
Should teach His brethren, and inspire
 To suffer and to die.

Praise to the Holiest in the height,
 And in the depth be praise,
In all His works most wonderful,
 Most sure in all His ways!

*Cardinal Newman, once an Anglican clergyman, engaged in much controversy
about Church matters. But he and all his opponents would have been in
complete agreement on the truth of the Christian religion as expressed in
this hymn, and they believed it literally, not as a fairy-tale or a metaphor.
Hard to imagine today.*

from
The Rubáiyát of Omar Khayyám   34

EDWARD FITZGERALD

Awake! for Morning in the Bowl of Night
Has flung the Stone that puts the Stars to Flight:
    And Lo! the Hunter of the East has caught
The Sultán's Turret in a Noose of Light.

Dreaming when Dawn's Left Hand was in the Sky
I heard a Voice within the Tavern cry,
    'Awake, my Little ones, and fill the Cup
Before Life's Liquor in its Cup be dry.'

And, as the Cock crew, those who stood before
The Tavern shouted – 'Open then the Door!
    You know how little while we have to stay,
And, once departed, may return no more.'

Come, fill the Cup, and in the Fire of Spring
The Winter Garment of Repentance fling:
    The Bird of Time has but a little way
To fly – and Lo! the Bird is on the Wing.

With me along some Strip of Herbage strown
That just divides the desert from the sown,
    Where name of slave and Sultán scarce is known,
And pity Sultán Máhmúd on his Throne.

Here with a Loaf of Bread beneath the Bough,
A Flask of Wine, a Book of Verse – and Thou
    Beside me singing in the Wilderness –
And Wilderness is Paradise enow.

'How sweet is mortal Sovranty!' – think some:
Others – 'How blest the Paradise to come!'
    Ah, take the Cash in hand and waive the Rest;
Oh, the brave Music of a *distant* Drum!

The Worldly Hope men set their Hearts upon
Turns Ashes – or it prospers; and anon,
    Like Snow upon the Desert's dusty Face
Lighting a little Hour or two – is gone.

Omar Khayyám ('Omar the Tentmaker') was a twelfth-century Persian
mathematician and astronomer who also wrote some hundreds of rubáiyát
(four-line verses or epigrams). FitzGerald translated, or freely adapted, a
selection of these and the result was enormously successful in all English-
speaking countries for many years.

The Recruit

A. E. HOUSMAN

Leave your home behind, lad,
　　And reach your friends your hand,
And go, and luck go with you
　　While Ludlow tower shall stand.

Oh, come you home of Sunday
　　When Ludlow streets are still
And Ludlow bells are calling
　　To farm and lane and mill,

Or come you home of Monday
　　When Ludlow market hums
And Ludlow chimes are playing
　　'The conquering hero comes',

Come you home a hero,
　　Or come not home at all,
The lads you leave will mind you
　　Till Ludlow tower shall fall.

And you will list the bugle
　　That blows in lands of morn,
And make the foes of England
　　Be sorry you were born.

And you till trump of doomsday
　　On lands of morn may lie,
And make the hearts of comrades
　　Be heavy where you die.

Leave your home behind you,
　　Your friends by field and town:
Oh, town and field will mind you
　　Till Ludlow tower is down.

Poems about battles and soldiering in general seem to have been written by
almost all the Victorian poets. It has been suggested that this was an indirect
way of working off sexual repression. However this might apply to Tennyson,
for instance, it is certainly worth considering in the case of Housman, a
bachelor don.

Goods Train at Night

KENNETH H. ASHLEY

The station is empty and desolate;
A sick lamp wanly glows;
Slowly puffs a goods engine,
Slow yet alive with great energy;
Drawing rumbling truck
After rumbling, rumbling truck;
Big, half-seen, insensate.
Yet each as it jolts through the glow
Responds to the questioning light,
Dumbly revealing
Diverse personality . . .
'Neal & Co.'; 'John Bugsworth'; 'Norland Collieries Limited';
'Jolly & Sons'; 'Jolly & Sons'; 'Jolly & Sons';
Thrice repeated, percussive, insistent –
Each wet wallside successively announcing
Names: badges and symbols of men,
Of men in their intricate trafficking –
But there quickens a deeper emotion,
Roused by the iterant names,
Beyond the mere intricate commerce,
The infinite wonder of life.
Effort and hope and love, the heart's desire,
Leap in the womb of the brain
As the trucks clang their way through the night.
Slides by the guard's van at the last,
With a last definite clatter of steel upon steel
And a glitter of ruby-red light.

So: silence recaptures the station;
The damp steam eddies out;
The drizzle weaves a silver pattern,
An endless shining silver pattern,
A silver woof in the lamplight.
And I find myself full of a grief –
A dull little grief for humanity.

This is that very rare thing, a poem in free verse that has a discernible rhythm
and momentum of its own. It also makes something poetic and haunting out of
very ordinary material. I can discover nothing about Kenneth H. Ashley except
that he published this poem in a magazine in London about sixty-six years ago.

37

Four Short Poems

ROBERT GRAVES

Dead Cow Farm

An ancient saga tells us how
In the beginning the First Cow
(For nothing living yet had birth
But Elemental Cow on earth)
Began to lick cold stones and mud:
Under her warm tongue flesh and blood
Blossomed, a miracle to believe:
And so was Adam born, and Eve.
Here now is chaos once again,
Primeval mud, cold stones and rain.
Here flesh decays and blood drips red,
And the Cow's dead, the old Cow's dead.

Cold Weather Proverb

Fearless approach and puffed feather
In birds, famine bespeak;
In man, belly filled full.

Love Without Hope

Love without hope, as when the young bird-catcher
Swept off his tall hat to the Squire's own daughter,
So let the imprisoned larks escape and fly
Singing about her head, as she rode by.

Flying Crooked

The butterfly, a cabbage-white,
(His honest idiocy of flight)
Will never now, it is too late,
Master the art of flying straight,
Yet has – who knows so well as I? –
A just sense of how not to fly:
He lurches here and here by guess
And God and hope and hopelessness.
Even the aerobatic swift
Has not his flying-crooked gift.

Graves never published a poem longer than a couple of pages and he always excelled at the very short kind that puts a single point in the fewest possible words. The earliest one here is 'Dead Cow Farm', written during the Great War when he was an officer in the Royal Welch Fusiliers on the Western Front.

Weary with Toil   38

WILLIAM SHAKESPEARE

Weary with toil, I haste me to my bed,
The dear repose for limbs with travel tired;
But then begins a journey in my head
To work my mind, when body's work's expir'd:
For then my thoughts, from far where I abide,
Intend a zealous pilgrimage to thee,
And keep my drooping eyelids open wide,
Looking on darkness which the blind do see:
Save that my soul's imaginary sight
Presents thy shadow to my sightless view,
Which, like a jewel hung in ghastly night,
Makes black night beauteous and her old face new.
        Lo! thus, by day my limbs, by night my mind,
        For thee and for myself no quiet find.

It is no wonder that, in the four centuries since Shakespeare wrote his sonnets, many words should have changed their meanings. This, plus the fact that the sonnets are about the most concentrated poems in the language, can make them difficult. But here all is plain – except perhaps that instead of 'shadow' we might nowadays say something like 'image' or 'mental picture'.

The Breaking

EDWIN MUIR

Peace in the western sky,
A ploughman follows the plough,
Children come home from school:
War is preparing now.

Great-grandfather on his farm
In eighteen hundred and ten
Heard of great victories
From wandering tinkermen,
Until the press-gang came,
Took son and servant away,
The fields were left forlorn
And there was nothing to say.
The farmer ploughed and reaped,
Led five lean harvests in,
The young men long away:
There was a great war then.
All things stand in their place
Till hatred beats them down,
Furies and fantasies
Strike flat the little town.
Then all rise up again,
But heart and blood and bone,
The very stones in the street,
Roof and foundation stone,
Remember and foreknow.
Memories, prophecies,
The song the ploughman sings,
The simple dream of peace,
Dark dreams in the dead of night
And on the reckless brow
Bent to let chaos in,
Tell that they shall come down,
Be broken, and rise again.

Muir never achieved the fame of his contemporaries Ezra Pound and T. S. Eliot,
but to some people he is more satisfying than either. This poem, found among
his papers after his death, is very characteristic in its steady, thoughtful tone
and its quiet acceptance of the way all things pass and yet are always renewed.

Kubla Khan

SAMUEL TAYLOR COLERIDGE

In Xanadu did KUBLA KHAN
A stately pleasure-dome decree:
Where ALPH, the sacred river, ran
Through caverns measureless to man
    Down to a sunless sea.
So twice five miles of fertile ground
With walls and towers were girdled round:
And here were gardens bright with sinuous rills,
Where blossomed many an incense-bearing tree,
And here were forests ancient as the hills,
Enfolding sunny spots of greenery.

But oh! that deep romantic chasm which slanted
Down the green hill athwart a cedarn cover!
A savage place! as holy and enchanted
As e'er beneath a waning moon was haunted
By woman wailing for her demon-lover!
And from this chasm, with ceaseless turmoil seething,
As if this earth in fast thick pants were breathing,
A mighty fountain momently was forced:
Amid whose swift half-intermitted burst
Huge fragments vaulted like rebounding hail,
Or chaffy grain beneath the thresher's flail;
And 'mid these dancing rocks at once and ever
It flung up momently the sacred river.
Five miles meandering with a mazy motion
Through wood and dale the sacred river ran,
Then reached the caverns measureless to man,
And sank in tumult to a lifeless ocean:
And 'mid this tumult Kubla heard from far
Ancestral voices prophesying war!

    The shadow of the dome of pleasure
    Floated midway on the waves;
    Where was heard the mingled measure
    From the fountain and the caves.
It was a miracle of rare device,
A sunny pleasure-dome with caves of ice!

    A damsel with a dulcimer
    In a vision once I saw:
    It was an Abyssinian maid,
    And on her dulcimer she play'd,
    Singing of Mount Abora.

[continued]

Could I revive within me
Her symphony and song,
To such a deep delight 'twould win me,
That with music loud and long,
I would build that dome in air,
That sunny dome! those caves of ice!
And all who heard should see them there,
And all should cry, Beware! Beware!
His flashing eyes, his floating hair!
Weave a circle round him thrice,
And close your eyes with holy dread,
For he on honey-dew hath fed,
And drunk the milk of Paradise.

Coleridge said he dreamt this as the first part of a longer poem which he was busy copying out when a caller at the door interrupted the flow and destroyed his memory of the remainder. A good story, impossible to disprove, and anyway what we have is a masterpiece, perhaps the most romantic poem in the language.

41   # The Indian Serenade

PERCY BYSSHE SHELLEY

I arise from dreams of thee
In the first sweet sleep of night,
When the winds are breathing low,
And the stars are shining bright;
I arise from dreams of thee,
And a spirit in my feet
Hath led me – who knows how?
To thy chamber-window, Sweet!

The wandering airs they faint
On the dark, the silent stream –
The Champak odours fail
Like sweet thoughts in a dream;
The nightingale's complaint,
It dies upon her heart,
As I must die on thine,
O belovèd as thou art!

O lift me from the grass!
I die! I faint! I fail!
Let thy love in kisses rain
On my lips and eyelids pale.
My cheek is cold and white, alas!
My heart beats loud and fast:
O press it to thine own again,
Where it will break at last!

Shelley was a very productive and also a very versatile poet. Some of his work is concerned with abstract ideas and is far from easy reading, but he also developed a talent for short romantic lyrics like this one. At that time the East (or the imagined East) was a relatively new subject. The Champak is the fragrant Indian magnolia.

The Lonely Farmer   42

R. S. THOMAS

Poor hill farmer astray in the grass:
There came a movement and he looked up, but
All that he saw was the wind pass.
There was a sound of voices on the air,
But where, where? It was only the glib stream talking
Softly to itself. And once when he was walking
Along a lane in spring he was deceived
By a shrill whistle coming through the leaves:
Wait a minute, wait a minute – four swift notes;
He turned, and it was nothing, only a thrush
In the thorn bushes easing its throat.
He swore at himself for paying heed,
The poor hill farmer, so often again
Stopping, staring, listening, in vain,
His ear betrayed by the heart's need.

As rector of a parish in the farming country of the Welsh hills, Thomas had the chance to get to know intimately the place and those living there, and he used it. Even so, it could not have been easy to write of them so directly and unsensationally. The grimness of the picture is relieved by the poet's compassion.

from
43 *A Satire against Reason and Mankind*

JOHN WILMOT, EARL OF ROCHESTER

Be Judge yourself, I'll bring it to the test,
Which is the basest Creature, Man or Beast?
Birds feed on Birds, Beasts on each other prey,
But Savage Man alone does Man betray:
Pressed by necessity, they Kill for Food,
Man undoes Man, to do himself no good.
With Teeth and Claws by Nature armed, they hunt
Nature's allowance, to supply their want,
But Man, with smiles, embraces, friendship, praise,
Inhumanly his Fellow's life betrays;
With voluntary pains works his distress,
Not through necessity but wantonness.
    For hunger or for Love they fight and tear,
Whilst wretched Man is still in Arms for fear;
For fear he arms, and is of Arms afraid,
By fear to fear successively betrayed,
Base fear, the source whence his best passions came,
His boasted Honour and his dear-bought Fame,
That lust of Power, to which he's such a Slave,
And for the which alone he dares be brave:
To which his various Projects are designed,
Which makes him generous, affable and kind,
For which he takes such pains to be thought wise,
And screws his actions in a forced disguise:
Leading a tedious life in Misery,
Under laborious, mean hypocrisy.
Look to the bottom of his vast design,
Wherein Man's Wisdom, Power and Glory join;
The good he acts, the ill he does endure,
'Tis all from fear, to make himself secure.
Merely for safety, after Fame we thirst
For all Men would be Cowards if they durst.
    And honesty's against all common sense,
Men must be Knaves, 'tis in their own defence.
Mankind's dishonest: if you think it fair,
Amongst known Cheats, to play upon the square,
You'll be undone . . .

Rochester was a favourite of Charles II, who often banished him from the court
but always had him back again. He lived a debauched and violent life and
wrote some amorous lyrics and satirical verses, all skilful, some obscene. This
satire is his best work, a savage but measured attack on man's inhumanity.

The Cottage Hospital

JOHN BETJEMAN

At the end of a long-walled garden
    in a red provincial town,
A brick path led to a mulberry –
    scanty grass at its feet.
I lay under blackening branches
    where the mulberry leaves hung down
Sheltering ruby fruit globes
    from a Sunday-tea-time heat.
Apple and plum espaliers
    basked upon bricks of brown;
The air was swimming with insects,
    and children played in the street.

Out of this bright intentness
    into the mulberry shade
Musca domestica (housefly)
    swung from the August light
Slap into slithery rigging
    by the waiting spider made
Which spun the lithe elastic
    till the fly was shrouded tight.
Down came the hairy talons
    and horrible poison blade
And none of the garden noticed
    that fizzing, hopeless fight.

Say in what Cottage Hospital
    whose pale green walls resound
With the tap upon polished parquet
    of inflexible nurses' feet
Shall I myself be lying
    when they range the screens around?
And say shall I groan in dying,
    as I twist the sweaty sheet?
Or gasp for breath uncrying,
    as I feel my senses drown'd
While the air is swimming with insects
    and children play in the street?

This dark, awesome poem reminds us that Sir John Betjeman was a cheerful character, a brilliant broadcaster and fascinating observer of our towns and churches as well as a writer of marvellously entertaining verse. He was all that but he was more than that: a poet as much in earnest as any there has been.

The Rabbit's Advice

ELIZABETH JENNINGS

I have been away too long.
Some of you think I am only a nursery tale,
One which you've grown out of.
Or perhaps you saw a movie and laughed at my ears
But rather envied my carrot.
I must tell you that I exist.

I'm a puff of wool leaping across a field,
Quick to all noises,
Smelling my burrow of safety.
I am easily frightened. A bird
Is tame compared to me.
Perhaps you have seen my fat white cousin who sits,
Constantly twitching his nose,
Behind bars in a hutch at the end of a garden.
If not, imagine those nights when you lie awake
Afraid to turn over, afraid
Of night and dawn and sleep.
Terror is what I am made
Of partly, partly of speed.

But I am a figure of fun.
I have no dignity
Which means I am never free.
So, when you are frightened or being teased, think of
My twitching whiskers, my absurd white puff of a tail,
Of all that I mean by 'me'
And my ludicrous craving for love.

The kind of animal poem in which the poet tries to imagine what it might be
like to be that animal has come along quite recently. There is nobody better at it
than Elizabeth Jennings. Inevitably, she says something about people as well
and the craving for love felt as much by the insignificant as by any.

Exposure

WILFRED OWEN

Our brains ache, in the merciless iced east winds that knive us . . .
Wearied we keep awake because the night is silent . . .
Low, drooping flares confuse our memory of the salient . . .
Worried by silence, sentries whisper, curious, nervous,
    But nothing happens.

Watching, we hear the mad gusts tugging on the wire,
Like twitching agonies of men among its brambles.
Northward, incessantly, the flickering gunnery rumbles,
Far off, like a dull rumour of some other war.
    What are we doing here?

The poignant misery of dawn begins to grow . . .
We only know war lasts, rain soaks, and clouds sag stormy.
Dawn massing in the east her melancholy army
Attacks once more in ranks on shivering ranks of gray,
    But nothing happens.

Sudden successive flights of bullets streak the silence.
Less deathly than the air that shudders black with snow,
With sidelong flowing flakes that flock, pause, and renew;
We watch them wandering up and down the wind's nonchalance,
    But nothing happens.

Pale flakes with fingering stealth come feeling for our faces –
We cringe in holes, back on forgotten dreams, and stare, snow-dazed,
Deep into grassier ditches. So we drowse, sun-dozed,
Littered with blossoms trickling where the blackbird fusses.
    Is it that we are dying?

Slowly our ghosts drag home: glimpsing the sunk fires, glozed
With crusted dark-red jewels; crickets jingle there;
For hours the innocent mice rejoice: the house is theirs;
Shutters and doors, all closed: on us the doors are closed –
    We turn back to our dying.

Since we believe not otherwise can kind fires burn;
Nor ever suns smile true on child, or field, or fruit.
For God's invincible spring our love is made afraid;
Therefore, not loath, we lie out here; therefore were born,
    For love of God seems dying.

[continued]

To-night, His frost will fasten on this mud and us,
Shrivelling many hands, puckering foreheads crisp.
The burying-party, picks and shovels in their shaking grasp,
Pause over half-known faces. All their eyes are ice,
    But nothing happens.

*This dates from the winter of 1917–18. Owen uses his reverse-rhymes (knive
us/nervous, wire/war, etc.) to great effect in one of the most powerful war
poems ever written. A salient was a part of the front line jutting into enemy-
held territory and so was specially dangerous. Gray: also the colour of German
uniforms.*

47

Adlestrop

EDWARD THOMAS

Yes, I remember Adlestrop –
The name, because one afternoon
Of heat the express-train drew up there
Unwontedly. It was late June.

The steam hissed. Someone cleared his throat.
No one left and no one came
On the bare platform. What I saw
Was Adlestrop – only the name.

And willows, willow-herb, and grass,
And meadowsweet, and haycocks dry,
No whit less still and lonely fair
Than the high cloudlets in the sky.

And for that minute a blackbird sang
Close by, and round him, mistier,
Farther and farther, all the birds
Of Oxfordshire and Gloucestershire.

*Thomas was killed in the Great War, not very long after suddenly discovering
he was a poet. Most of his poems are about the countryside, brief close glimpses
of a single scene or a moment, unsensational, unpretentious, so cunningly
crafted that it all seems spontaneous. Alas, there is no station at Adlestrop now.*

On the Death of Mr Robert Levet, 48
a Practiser in Physic

SAMUEL JOHNSON

Condemn'd to hope's delusive mine,
   As on we toil from day to day,
By sudden blasts, or slow decline,
   Our social comforts drop away.

Well tried through many a varying year,
   See LEVET to the grave descend;
Officious, innocent, sincere,
   Of ev'ry friendless name the friend.

Yet still he fills affection's eye,
   Obscurely wise, and coarsely kind;
Nor, letter'd arrogance, deny
   Thy praise to merit unrefin'd.

When fainting nature call'd for aid,
   And hov'ring death prepar'd the blow,
His vig'rous remedy display'd
   The power of art without the show.

In misery's darkest caverns known,
   His useful care was ever nigh,
Where hopeless anguish pour'd his groan,
   And lonely want retir'd to die.

No summons mock'd by chill delay,
   No petty gain disdain'd by pride,
The modest wants of ev'ry day
   The toil of ev'ry day supplied.

His virtues walk'd their narrow round,
   Nor made a pause, nor left a void;
And sure th'Eternal Master found
   The single talent well employ'd.

The busy day, the peaceful night,
   Unfelt, uncounted, glided by;
His frame was firm, his powers were bright,
   Tho' now his eightieth year was nigh.

[continued]

Then with no throbbing fiery pain,
No cold gradations of decay,
Death broke at once the vital chain,
And free'd his soul the nearest way.

*Johnson was in his middle seventies himself when he wrote this graceful tribute
to a family doctor (a GP as we would now call him). His praise is the more
effective because it is carefully weighed; nothing is exaggerated and there are no
wails of grief. In the eighteenth century, 'officious' meant kind, considerate.*

49 Go Where Glory Waits Thee

THOMAS MOORE

Go where glory waits thee,
But while fame elates thee,
    Oh! still remember me.
When the praise thou meetest
To thine ear is sweetest,
    Oh! then remember me.
Other arms may press thee,
Dearer friends caress thee,
All the joys that bless thee,
    Sweeter far may be;
But when friends are nearest,
And when joys are dearest,
    Oh! then remember me.

When at eve thou rovest,
By the star thou lovest,
    Oh! then remember me.
Think, when home returning,
Bright we've seen it burning;
    Oh! thus remember me.
Oft as summer closes,
When thine eye reposes
On its ling'ring roses.
    Once so lov'd by thee,
Think of her who wove them,
Her who made thee love them,
    Oh! then remember me.

When, around thee dying,
Autumn leaves are lying,
   Oh! then remember me.
And at night when gazing
On the gay hearth blazing,
   Oh! still remember me.
Then, should music stealing
All the soul of feeling,
To thy heart appealing,
   Draw one tear from thee;
Then let memory bring thee
Strains I us'd to sing thee, –
   Oh! then remember me.

Moore's lyrics run so smoothly and seem so inevitable in their phrasing that it is easy to overlook the skill with which the words are chosen and fitted together. No one ever beat him in the writing of simple, romantic, sentimental, ballad-like poems suitable for musical setting, sometimes supplied by himself.

Remember

50

CHRISTINA ROSSETTI

Remember me when I am gone away,
   Gone far away into the silent land;
   When you can no more hold me by the hand,
Nor I half turn to go yet turning stay.
Remember me when no more day by day
   You tell me of our future that you planned:
   Only remember me; you understand
It will be late to counsel then or pray.
Yet if you should forget me for a while
   And afterwards remember, do not grieve:
   For if the darkness and corruption leave
   A vestige of the thoughts that once I had,
Better by far you should forget and smile
   Than that you should remember and be sad.

Christina Rossetti is the finest of our women poets. She was a deeply religious High-Church Anglican who never married, refusing two suitors on conscientious grounds. This poem is addressed to the first of these, from whom she parted with great sorrow.

51   The Ballad of Sally in our Alley

HENRY CAREY

Of all the Girls that are so smart
    There's none like pretty Sally,
She is the Darling of my Heart,
    And she lives in our Alley.
There is no Lady in the Land,
    Is half so sweet as Sally,
She is the Darling of my Heart,
    And she lives in our Alley.

. . . . . .

When she is by I leave my Work,
    (I love her so sincerely)
My Master comes like any Turk,
    And bangs me most severely;
But, let him bang his Belly-full,
    I'll bear it all for Sally;
She is the Darling of my Heart,
    And she lives in our Alley.

Of all the Days that's in the Week,
    I dearly love but one Day,
And that's the Day that comes betwixt
    A Saturday and Monday;
For then I'm dress'd, all in my best,
    To walk abroad with Sally:
She is the Darling of my Heart,
    And she lives in our Alley.

. . . . . .

My Master and the Neighbours all
    Make game of me and Sally;
And (but for her) I'd better be
    A Slave and row a Galley:
But when my seven long Years are out,
    O then I'll marry Sally!
O then we'll wed and then we'll bed,
    But not in our Alley.

*Henry Carey was a poet and musician who wrote mostly for the stage. This is
the best-remembered of his songs. He wrote a tune for it but this was later
discarded. The story goes that it was Carey who, in 1740, first sang a version of
'God Save the King' at a tavern near London Bridge.*

A Sea-Song

ALLAN CUNNINGHAM

A wet sheet and a flowing sea,
   A wind that follows fast
And fills the white and rustling sail
   And bends the gallant mast;
And bends the gallant mast, my boys,
   While like the eagle free
Away the good ship flies, and leaves
   Old England on the lee.

O for a soft and gentle wind!
   I heard a fair one cry:
But give to me the snoring breeze
   And white waves heaving high;
And white waves heaving high, my lads,
   The good ship tight and free –
The world of waters is our home,
   And merry men are we.

There's tempest in yon hornèd moon,
   And lightning in yon cloud;
But hark the music, mariners!
   The wind is piping loud;
The wind is piping loud, my boys,
   The lightning flashes free –
While the hollow oak our palace is,
   Our heritage the sea.

Cunningham was a Scot with an interest in folk tales and ballads. This famous
song is very much of its period, the early nineteenth century, when Britain was
a great and expanding naval power. And yet with the present spreading interest
in yachting and boating of all sorts it may still mean something.

53

Abou Ben Adhem

JAMES LEIGH HUNT

Abou Ben Adhem (may his tribe increase!)
Awoke one night from a deep dream of peace,
And saw, within the moonlight in his room,
Making it rich, and like a lily in bloom,
An angel writing in a book of gold:
Exceeding peace had made Ben Adhem bold,
And to the presence in the room he said,
   'What writest thou?' – The vision raised its head,
And with a look made of all sweet accord,
Answered, 'The names of those who love the Lord.'
'And is mine one?' said Abou. 'Nay, not so,'
Replied the angel. Abou spoke more low,
But cheerly still; and said, 'I pray thee, then,
Write me as one that loves his fellow men.'
   The angel wrote, and vanished. The next night
It came again with a great wakening light,
And showed the names whom love of God had blest,
And lo! Ben Adhem's name led all the rest.

James Henry Leigh Hunt was a journalist and editor, once imprisoned for a libel on the Prince Regent. Most of his work was in the essay form, but he produced a handful of poems for which he is still remembered. This is the best-known of them.

Sudden Light

DANTE GABRIEL ROSSETTI

I have been here before,
But when or how I cannot tell:
I know the grass beyond the door,
The sweet keen smell,
The sighing sound, the lights around the shore.

You have been mine before, –
How long ago I may not know:
But just when at that swallow's soar
Your neck turned so,
Some veil did fall, – I knew it all of yore.

Then, now – perchance again! . . .
O round mine eyes your tresses shake!
Shall we not lie as we have lain
Thus for Love's sake,
And sleep, and wake, yet never break the chain?

Rossetti and his sister, Christina, our finest woman poet, were born in London
of Italian émigré parents. In his early years he was known chiefly as a painter,
being a founder-member of the Pre-Raphaelite movement, but was later
successful as a poet too. Here he captures the mysterious feeling of déjà vu
that most people have experienced at some point in their lives.

from
Milton

WILLIAM BLAKE

And did those feet in ancient time
　　Walk upon England's mountains green?
And was the holy Lamb of God
　　On England's pleasant pastures seen?

And did the Countenance Divine
　　Shine forth upon our clouded hills?
And was Jerusalem builded here
　　Among these dark Satanic Mills?

Bring me my Bow of burning gold:
　　Bring me my Arrows of desire:
Bring me my Spear: O clouds unfold!
　　Bring me my Chariot of fire!

I will not cease from Mental Fight,
　　Nor shall my Sword sleep in my hand,
Till we have built Jerusalem
In England's green and pleasant Land.

If you know any poems at all the odds are you know this one. Not much to say, except this: there is evidence that it is a call not for a better, cleaner world but for sexual freedom, and by dark satanic mills Blake meant not factories and sweat-shops but church altars. If true, a fine irony.

The Sands of Dee

CHARLES KINGSLEY

'O Mary, go and call the cattle home,
    And call the cattle home,
    And call the cattle home
  Across the sands of Dee';
The western wind was wild and dank with foam,
    And all alone went she.

The western tide crept up along the sand,
    And o'er and o'er the sand,
    And round and round the sand,
  As far as eye could see.
The rolling mist came down and hid the land:
    And never home came she.

'Oh! is it weed, or fish, or floating hair –
    A tress of golden hair,
    A drownèd maiden's hair
  Above the nets at sea?
Was never salmon yet that shone so fair
    Among the stakes on Dee.'

They rowed her in across the rolling foam,
    The cruel crawling foam,
    The cruel hungry foam,
  To her grave beside the sea;
But still the boatmen hear her call the cattle home
  Across the sands of Dee.

Kingsley was a country parson in Hampshire, an early socialist and a novelist and story-teller as well as a poet, with the unique distinction of having a town named after one of his books – Westward Ho! in North Devon. The ballad-like style of this poem is quite characteristic.

57 *All the World's a Stage*

WILLIAM SHAKESPEARE

All the world's a stage,
And all the men and women merely players:
They have their exits and their entrances;
And one man in his time plays many parts,
His acts being seven ages. At first the infant,
Mewling and puking in the nurse's arms,
And then the whining schoolboy, with his satchel,
And shining morning face, creeping like snail
Unwillingly to school. And then the lover,
Sighing like furnace, with a woeful ballad
Made to his mistress' eyebrow. Then a soldier,
Full of strange oaths, and bearded like the pard,
Jealous in honour, sudden and quick in quarrel,
Seeking the bubble reputation
Even in the cannon's mouth. And then the justice,
In fair round belly with good capon lined,
With eyes severe and beard of formal cut,
Full of wise saws and modern instances;
And so he plays his part. The sixth age shifts
Into the lean and slippered pantaloon,
With spectacles on nose, and pouch on side,
His youthful hose, well saved, a world too wide
For his shrunk shank; and his big manly voice,
Turning again toward childish treble, pipes
And whistles in his sound. Last scene of all,
That ends this strange eventful history,
Is second childishness and mere oblivion,
Sans teeth, sans eyes, sans taste, sans everything.

This speech of the courtier Jaques in As You Like It used to be known at least
in part by just about everybody who could read and write. I very much doubt if
it still is. But even if I am wrong there cannot be many people who will object to
being reminded of it.

Non sum qualis eram bonae sub regno Cynarae

ERNEST DOWSON

Last night, ah, yesternight, betwixt her lips and mine
There fell thy shadow, Cynara! thy breath was shed
Upon my soul between the kisses and the wine;
And I was desolate and sick of an old passion,
    Yea, I was desolate and bowed my head:
I have been faithful to thee, Cynara! in my fashion.

All night upon mine heart I felt her warm heart beat,
Night-long within mine arms in love and sleep she lay;
Surely the kisses of her bought red mouth were sweet;
But I was desolate and sick of an old passion,
    When I awoke and found the dawn was gray:
I have been faithful to thee, Cynara! in my fashion.

I have forgot much, Cynara! gone with the wind,
Flung roses, roses riotously with the throng,
Dancing, to put thy pale, lost lilies out of mind;
But I was desolate and sick of an old passion,
    Yea, all the time, because the dance was long:
I have been faithful to thee, Cynara! in my fashion.

I cried for madder music and for stronger wine,
But when the feast is finished and the lamps expire,
Then falls thy shadow, Cynara! the night is thine;
And I am desolate and sick of an old passion,
    Yea, hungry for the lips of my desire:
I have been faithful to thee, Cynara! in my fashion.

Dowson belongs to the 'Nineties, that period of supposed dissipation and artistic exuberance at the end of the Victorian era. In his short life he published two books of poems, of which this is almost the only one still to be remembered. The title of a famous book and a film was taken from it.

59 Home-Thoughts, from Abroad

ROBERT BROWNING

Oh, to be in England
Now that April's there,
And whoever wakes in England
Sees, some morning, unaware,
That the lowest boughs and the brushwood sheaf
Round the elm-tree bole are in tiny leaf,
While the chaffinch sings on the orchard bough
In England – now!

And after April, when May follows,
And the whitethroat builds, and all the swallows!
Hark, where my blossomed pear-tree in the hedge
Leans to the field and scatters on the clover
Blossoms and dewdrops – at the bent spray's edge –
That's the wise thrush; he sings each song twice over,
Lest you should think he never could recapture
The first fine careless rapture!
And though the fields look rough with hoary dew,
All will be gay when noontide wakes anew
The buttercups, the little children's dower
– Far brighter than this gaudy melon-flower!

Browning lived in Italy for some years but this poem, which reads like an exile's
postcard home, was actually written before he settled there. As well as a
marvellous eye (and ear) it shows how he would make up his own arrangement
of rhyme and metre to suit what he had to say. 'Careless rapture' is his phrase,
not Ivor Novello's.

There Is a Lady Sweet and Kind 60

THOMAS FORD

There is a Lady sweet and kind,
Was never face so pleas'd my mind;
I did but see her passing by,
And yet I love her till I die.

Her gesture, motion and her smiles,
Her wit, her voyce, my heart beguiles,
Beguiles my heart, I know not why,
And yet I love her till I die.

Her free behaviour, winning lookes,
Will make a Lawyer burne his bookes.
I touch'd her not, alas, not I,
And yet I love her till I die.

Had I her fast betwixt mine armes,
Judge you that thinke such sports were harmes,
Wer't any harm? no, no, fie, fie!
For I will love her till I die.

Should I remaine confined there,
So long as Phebus in his sphere,
I to request, she to denie,
Yet would I love her till I die.

Cupid is wingèd and doth range,
Her countrie so my love doth change,
But change she earth, or change she skie,
Yet will I love her till I die.

Not much more is known about Ford that that he was a court musician and
that he wrote this, or at any rate wrote it down. The poem was known for
generations in a sort of non-alcoholic version consisting only of the first, second
and last verses, the earthier but no less appealing ones omitted.

Moonlit Apples

JOHN DRINKWATER

At the top of the house the apples are laid in rows,
And the skylight lets the moonlight in, and those
Apples are deep-sea apples of green. There goes
    A cloud on the moon in the autumn night.

A mouse in the wainscot scratches, and scratches, and then
There is no sound at the top of the house of men
Or mice; and the cloud is blown, and the moon again
    Dapples the apples with deep-sea light.

They are lying in rows there, under the gloomy beams;
On the sagging floor; they gather the silver streams
Out of the moon, those moonlit apples of dreams,
    And quiet is the steep stair under.

In the corridors under there is nothing but sleep.
And stiller than ever on orchard boughs they keep
Tryst with the moon, and deep is the silence, deep
    On moon-washed apples of wonder.

Like many poets of his time, John Drinkwater aimed at revealing the qualities of wonder and strangeness in simple things that are usually taken for granted. This picture of apples stored in a farmhouse attic is very characteristic of his work.

The West Wind

JOHN MASEFIELD

It's a warm wind, the west wind, full of birds' cries;
I never hear the west wind but tears are in my eyes.
For it comes from the west lands, the old brown hills,
And April's in the west wind, and daffodils.

It's a fine land, the west land, for hearts as tired as mine,
Apple orchards blossom there, and the air's like wine,
There is cool green grass there, where men may lie at rest,
And the thrushes are in song there, fluting from the nest.

'Will you not come home, brother? you have been long away,
It's April, and blossom time, and white is the may;
And bright is the sun, brother, and warm is the rain, –
Will you not come home, brother, home to us again?

'The young corn is green, brother, where the rabbits run,
It's blue sky, and white clouds, and warm rain and sun.
It's song to a man's soul, brother, fire to a man's brain,
To hear the wild bees and see the merry spring again.

'Larks are singing in the west, brother, above the green wheat,
So will you not come home, brother, and rest your tired feet?
I've a balm for bruised hearts, brother, sleep for aching eyes,'
Says the warm wind, the west wind, full of birds' cries.

*Masefield was Poet Laureate for the last 37 years of his long life. Some of his
work is faded now, but he was always a good craftsman and at his best
communicated simply and effectively his love of the sea (he sailed to Chile in a
windjammer at the age of fifteen) and the open air. He was born in the West of
England.*

63

Women

HEATH

These women all
Both great and small
    Are wavering to and fro,
Now here, now there,
Now everywhere;
    But I will not say so.

So they love to range,
Their minds doth change
    And make their friend their foe;
As lovers true
Each day they choose new;
    But I will not say so.

They laugh, they smile,
They do beguile,
    As dice that men doth throw.
Who useth them much
Shall never be rich;
    But I will not say so.

Some hot, some cold,
There is no hold
    But as the wind doth blow;
When all is done,
They change like the moon;
    But I will not say so.

So thus one and other
Taketh after their mother,
    As cock by kind doth crow.
My song is ended,
The best may be amended;
    But I will not say so.

Nobody seems to know as much as Heath's Christian name, but it seems there is reason to believe that he lived in the reign of Henry VIII. There is also reason to believe that some things have not changed very much since Heath's day, but I will not say what.

To Marguerite

MATTHEW ARNOLD

Yes! in the sea of life enisled
With echoing straits between us thrown,
Dotting the shoreless watery wild,
We mortal millions live *alone*.
The islands feel the enclasping flow,
And then their endless bounds they know.

But when the moon their hollows lights,
And they are swept by balms of spring,
And in their glens, on starry nights,
The nightingales divinely sing;
And lovely notes, from shore to shore,
Across the sounds and channels pour –

Oh! then a longing like despair
Is to their farthest caverns sent;
For surely once, they feel, we were
Parts of a single continent!
Now round us spreads the watery plain –
Oh might our marges meet again!

Who order'd, that their longing's fire
Should be, as soon as kindled, cool'd?
Who renders vain their deep desire? –
A God, a God their severance ruled!
And bade betwixt their shores to be
The unplumb'd, salt, estranging sea.

I have often thought that Arnold could dig deeper than either of his two great
contemporaries, Tennyson and Browning. One of his recurrent themes is
human loneliness, the fact that we are all cut off from one another not by choice
but by circumstances of our existence. Every man is an island, he says here.

65

The Royal George

WILLIAM COWPER

Toll for the Brave!
  The brave that are no more!
All sunk beneath the wave
  Fast by their native shore!

Eight hundred of the brave,
  Whose courage well was tried,
Had made the vessel heel
  And laid her on her side.

A land-breeze shook the shrouds
  And she was overset;
Down went the Royal George
  With all her crew complete.

Toll for the brave!
  Brave Kempenfelt is gone;
His last sea-fight is fought,
  His work of glory done.

It was not in the battle;
  No tempest gave the shock;
She sprang no fatal leak,
  She ran upon no rock.

His sword was in its sheath,
  His fingers held the pen,
When Kempenfelt went down
  With twice four hundred men.

Weigh the vessel up
  Once dreaded by our foes!
And mingle with your cup
  The tears that England owes.

Her timbers yet are sound,
  And she may float again
Full charged with England's thunder,
  And plough the distant main:

> But Kempenfelt is gone,
>   His victories are o'er;
> And he and his eight hundred
>   Must plough the wave no more.

Admiral Kempenfelt (of Swedish descent) went down with his men in Portsmouth harbour in 1782. According to the official account, the hull of the Royal George was overloaded and collapsed. However, Cowper's poem helped to inaugurate a style of patriotic verse that became popular in the nineteenth century.

The Latest Decalogue   66

ARTHUR HUGH CLOUGH

Thou shalt have one God only; who
Would be at the expense of two?
No graven images may be
Worshipped, except the currency:
Swear not at all; for, for thy curse
Thine enemy is none the worse:
At church on Sunday to attend
Will serve to keep the world thy friend:
Honour thy parents; that is, all
From whom advancement may befall:
Thou shalt not kill; but need'st not strive
Officiously to keep alive:
Do not adultery commit;
Advantage rarely comes of it:
Thou shalt not steal; an empty feat,
When it's so lucrative to cheat:
Bear not false witness, let the lie
Have time on its own wings to fly:
Thou shalt not covet; but tradition
Approves all forms of competition.

Although Clough seems not to have been a strongly religious man, he launches here a bitter attack on the materialism of Victorian life by producing a travestied version of the Ten Commandments as followed by his contemporaries – this, he says, is what you live by. It is a splendid piece of calculated irony.

67

This Is the Key

ANONYMOUS

This is the key of the kingdom:
In that kingdom there is a city.
In that city there is a town.
In that town there is a street.
In that street there is a lane.
In that lane there is a yard.
In that yard there is a house.
In that house there is a room.
In that room there is a bed.
On that bed there is a basket.
In that basket there are some flowers.
Flowers in a basket.
Basket in the bed.
Bed in the room.
Room in the house.
House in the yard.
Yard in the lane.
Lane in the street.
Street in the town.
Town in the city.
City in the kingdom.
Of the kingdom this is the key.

This mysterious piece is perhaps not a poem at all. It seems to be full of meaning and yet to keep that meaning hidden. I cannot explain it, but I notice that everything up to and including the basket is the work of human beings. Not so the flowers.

A Slice of Wedding Cake 68

ROBERT GRAVES

Why have such scores of lovely, gifted girls
    Married impossible men?
Simple self-sacrifice may be ruled out,
    And missionary endeavour, nine times out of ten.

Repeat 'impossible men': not merely rustic,
    Foul-tempered or depraved
(Dramatic foils chosen to show the world
    How well women behave, and always have behaved).

Impossible men: idle, illiterate,
    Self-pitying, dirty, sly,
For whose appearance even in City parks
    Excuses must be made to casual passers-by.

Has God's supply of tolerable husbands
    Fallen, in fact, so low?
Or do I always over-value woman
    At the expense of man?
            Do I?
                It might be so.

*Best known, I suppose, as the author of I, Claudius, Graves has written a great
deal about the classical past and mythology. And yet he is about the only poet
of his generation who can write easily and naturally about everyday life and its
interests. The dry tone of this poem, and the sting in its tail, are quite typical.*

Peace

HENRY VAUGHAN

My soul, there is a country
   Far beyond the stars,
Where stands a winged sentry
   All skilful in the wars.

There, above noise and danger,
   Sweet peace sits crown'd with smiles,
And one born in a manger
   Commands the beauteous files.

He is thy gracious friend
   And (O my soul, awake!)
Did in pure love descend
   To die here for thy sake.

If thou canst get but thither,
   There grows the flower of peace,
The rose that cannot wither,
   Thy fortress, and thy ease.

Leave then thy foolish ranges;
   For none can thee secure,
But one, who never changes,
   Thy God, thy life, thy cure.

Henry Vaughan was born near the town of Usk in what is now Gwent and practised as a medical doctor in Wales. He was devoted to the beauties of the countryside and had a mystical feeling for nature. Sometimes, as here, he produced religious poetry of great simplicity.

Report on Experience

EDMUND BLUNDEN

I have been young, and now am not too old;
And I have seen the righteous forsaken,
His health, his honour and his quality taken.
    This is not what we were formally told.

I have seen a green country, useful to the race,
Knocked silly with guns and mines, its villages vanished,
Even the last rat and last kestrel banished –
    God bless us all, this was peculiar grace.

I knew Seraphina; Nature gave her hue,
Glance, sympathy, note, like one from Eden.
I saw her smile warp, heard her lyric deaden;
    She turned to harlotry – this I took to be new.

Say what you will, our God sees how they run.
These disillusions are His curious proving
That He loves humanity and will go on loving;
    Over there are faith, life, virtue in the sun.

*Blunden was a mild-mannered Oxford don whose usual poetical subject was
the English countryside. Any mildness in this poem is deceptive. In
unsensational language it catches those horrible moments when we realise that
life is not run as it should be. The second verse has some connection with
Blunden's service in France in the Great War.*

A Red, Red Rose

ROBERT BURNS

O, my luve's like a red, red rose
    That's newly sprung in June:
O, my luve's like the melodie
    That's sweetly play'd in tune.

As fair art thou, my bonnie lass,
    So deep in luve am I:
And I will luve thee still, my dear,
    Till a' the seas gang dry.

Till a' the seas gang dry, my dear,
    And the rocks melt wi' the sun:
And I will luve thee still, my dear,
    While the sands o' life shall run.

And fare thee weel, my only luve,
    And fare thee weel a while!
And I will come again, my luve,
    Tho' it were ten thousand mile.

It is part of the hard luck of the English that one of the greatest poets ever to be seen in these islands wrote most of his best work in broad Scots. But some, like today's poem, is straightforward enough – in fact this speaks so directly to the reader that one can hardly believe it was written nearly 200 years ago.

The Passionate Shepherd to His Love

CHRISTOPHER MARLOWE

Come live with me and be my love,
And we will all the pleasures prove,
That hills and valleys, dales and fields,
And all the craggy mountains yields.

There we will sit upon the rocks,
And see the shepherds feed their flocks,
By shallow rivers to whose falls
Melodious birds sing madrigals.

And I will make thee beds of roses
With a thousand fragrant posies,
A cap of flowers, and a kirtle
Embroidered all with leaves of myrtle;

A gown made of the finest wool
Which from our pretty lambs we pull;
Fair lined slippers for the cold,
With buckles of the purest gold;

A belt of straw and ivy buds,
With coral clasps and amber studs:
And if these pleasures may thee move,
Come live with me and be my love.

The shepherds' swains shall dance and sing
For thy delight each May morning:
If these delights thy mind may move,
Then live with me and be my love.

Marlowe is chiefly remembered today for his plays and translations. This poem, the only one of its kind he ever wrote, was not published until after he had died in a tavern brawl at the age of 29. For years it was very popular and inspired all manner of imitations and answers. One of these answers follows.

The Nymph's Reply to the Shepherd

SIR WALTER RALEGH

If all the world and love were young,
And truth in every shepherd's tongue,
These pretty pleasures might me move
To live with thee and be thy love.

Time drives the flocks from field to fold,
When rivers rage and rocks grow cold,
And Philomel becometh dumb;
The rest complain of cares to come.

The flowers do fade, and wanton fields
To wayward winter reckoning yields;
A honey tongue, a heart of gall,
Is fancy's spring, but sorrow's fall.

Thy gowns, thy shoes, thy beds of roses,
Thy cap, thy kirtle, and thy posies
Soon break, soon wither, soon forgotten,
In folly ripe, in reason rotten.

Thy belt of straw and ivy buds,
Thy coral clasps and amber studs,
All these in me no means can move
To come to thee and be thy love.

But could youth last and love still breed,
Had joys no date nor age no need,
Then these delights my mind might move
To live with thee and be thy love.

The Sir Walter who (probably) wrote this poem is the same one who went on expeditions to America, was imprisoned in the Tower of London and was finally executed. If he had led a less adventurous life his poetry might be better known.

The Captive Dove

ANNE BRONTË

Poor restless Dove, I pity thee,
    And when I hear thy plaintive moan
I mourn for thy captivity
    And in thy woes forget mine own.

To see thee stand prepared to fly,
    And flap those useless wings of thine,
And gaze into the distant sky
    Would melt a harder heart than mine.

In Vain! In Vain! Thou canst not rise –
    Thy prison roof confines thee there;
Its slender wires delude thine eyes,
    And quench thy longing with despair.

O! thou wert made to wander free
    In sunny mead and shady grove,
And far beyond the rolling sea
    In distant climes at will to rove.

Yet hadst thou but one gentle mate
    Thy little drooping heart to cheer
And share with thee thy captive state,
    Thou could'st be happy even there.

Yes, even there, if listening by
    One faithful dear companion stood,
While gazing on her full bright eye
    Thou might'st forget thy native wood.

But thou, poor solitary dove,
    Must make unheard thy joyless moan;
The heart that nature formed to love
    Must pine neglected and alone.

All the three Brontë sisters wrote novels and verse from an early age, partly as a distraction from their joyless and unhealthy life at Haworth Parsonage, near Bradford, with no mother, a drunken brother and an eccentric recluse of a father. In this poem by Anne, the youngest, the longing for escape is all too clear.

To Daffodils

ROBERT HERRICK

Fair Daffodils, we weep to see
　　You haste away so soon:
As yet the early-rising sun
　　Has not attained his noon.
　　　　Stay, stay,
　　Until the hasting day
　　　　Has run
　　But to the Evensong;
And, having prayed together, we
　　Will go with you along.

We have short time to stay as you,
　　We have as short a spring;
As quick a growth to meet decay,
　　As you, or anything.
　　　　We die,
　　As your hours do, and dry
　　　　Away
　　Like to the summer's rain;
Or as the pearls of morning's dew,
　　Ne'er to be found again.

In Herrick we have another parson-poet, a remarkable unstuffy one much given to love-lyrics. In this poem he draws a parallel between the few spring weeks when daffodils grow and the shortness of human life, a thought to be found in the work of other poets, but never handled in a more graceful or concentrated way.

The Power of Music

THOMAS LISLE

When Orpheus went down to the regions below,
    Which men are forbidden to see,
He tuned up his lyre, as old histories show,
    To set his Eurydice free.

All hell was astonished a person so wise
    Should rashly endanger his life,
And venture so far – but how vast their surprise
    When they heard that he came for his wife.

To find out a punishment due to his fault
    Old Pluto had puzzled his brain;
But hell had no torments sufficient, he thought,
    So gave him his wife back again.

But pity succeeding found place in his heart,
    And, pleased with his playing so well,
He took her again in reward of his art;
    Such power hath music in hell!

*I can find out nothing at all about Lisle except his dates. It was common
practice among the educated men of his time to take bits of classical mythology
like the legend of Orpheus in the underworld and produce comic variations of
them. I hope no wives will seriously object to this one.*

Composed upon Westminster Bridge

WILLIAM WORDSWORTH

77

Earth has not anything to show more fair:
Dull would he be of soul who could pass by
A sight so touching in its majesty:
This City now doth, like a garment, wear
The beauty of the morning; silent, bare,
Ships, towers, domes, theatres, and temples lie
Open unto the fields, and to the sky;
All bright and glittering in the smokeless air.
Never did sun more beautifully steep
In his first splendour, valley, rock or hill;
Ne'er saw I, never felt, a calm so deep!
The river glideth at his own sweet will:
Dear God! the very houses seem asleep;
And all that mighty heart is lying still!

When he wrote it in 1802, Wordsworth's famous sonnet had an originality not easy to recapture today. In his time it was the countryside that had pleasant descriptive poems written about it; town scenes were generally shown as ugly or squalid. He broke that tradition. (The bridge he stood on was replaced by the present structure about 1860.)

Danny Deever

RUDYARD KIPLING

'What are the bugles blowin' for?' said Files-on-Parade.
'To turn you out, to turn you out,' the Colour-Sergeant said.
'What makes you look so white, so white?' said Files-on-Parade.
'I'm dreadin' what I've got to watch,' the Colour-Sergeant said.
    For they're hangin' Danny Deever, you can hear the Dead March play,
    The Regiment's in 'ollow square – they're hangin' him to-day;
    They've taken of his buttons off an' cut his stripes away,
    An' they're hangin' Danny Deever in the mornin'.

'What makes the rear-rank breathe so 'ard?' said Files-on-Parade.
'It's bitter cold, it's bitter cold,' the Colour-Sergeant said.
'What makes that front-rank man fall down?' said Files-on-Parade.
'A touch o' sun, a touch o' sun,' the Colour-Sergeant said.
    They are hangin' Danny Deever, they are marchin' of 'im round,
    They 'ave 'alted Danny Deever by 'is coffin on the ground;
    An' 'e'll swing in 'arf a minute for a sneakin' shootin' hound –
    O they're hangin' Danny Deever in the mornin'!

' 'Is cot was right-'and cot to mine,' said Files-on-Parade.
' 'E's sleepin' out an' far to-night,' the Colour-Sergeant said.
'I've drunk 'is beer a score o' times,' said Files-on-Parade.
' 'E's drinkin' bitter beer alone,' the Colour-Sergeant said.
    They are hangin' Danny Deever, you must mark 'im to 'is place,
    For 'e shot a comrade sleepin' – you must look 'im in the face;
    Nine 'undred of 'is county an' the Regiment's disgrace,
    While they're hangin' Danny Deever in the mornin'.

'What's that so black agin the sun?', said Files-on-Parade.
'It's Danny fightin' 'ard for life', the Colour-Sergeant said.
'What's that that whimpers over 'ead?' said Files-on-Parade.
'It's Danny's soul that's passin' now,' the Colour-Sergeant said.
    For they're done with Danny Deever, you can 'ear the quickstep play,
    The Regiment's in column, an' they're marchin' us away;
    Ho! the young recruits are shakin', 'an' they'll want their beer to-day,
    After hangin' Danny Deever in the mornin'!

Without ever having served in it, Kipling knew the British Army inside out –
not so much the official side or the officers' side as the side of the rank and file,
the squaddies. He knew about the frightening bits, the boredom, the squalor
and the moments of pride. Also, as in this poem, what were seen as terrible
necessities.

79

Come Down, O Maid

ALFRED LORD TENNYSON

Come down, O maid, from yonder mountain height:
What pleasure lives in height (the shepherd sang)
In height and cold, the splendour of the hills?
But cease to move so near the Heavens, and cease
To glide a sunbeam by the blasted Pine,
To sit a star upon the sparkling spire;
And come, for Love is of the valley, come,
For Love is of the valley, come thou down
And find him; by the happy threshold, he,
Or hand in hand with Plenty in the maize
Or red with spirted purple of the vats,
Or foxlike in the vine; nor cares to walk
With Death and Morning on the silver horns,
Nor wilt thou snare him in the white ravine,
Nor find him dropt upon the firths of ice,
That huddling slant in furrow-cloven falls
To roll the torrent out of dusky doors:
But follow; let the torrent dance thee down
To find him in the valley; let the wild
Lean-headed Eagles yelp alone, and leave
The monstrous ledges there to slope, and spill
Their thousand wreaths of dangling water-smoke,
That like a broken purpose waste in air;
So waste not thou; but come; for all the vales
Await thee; azure pillars of the hearth
Arise to thee; the children call, and I
Thy shepherd pipe, and sweet is every sound,
Sweeter thy voice, but every sound is sweet,
Myriads of rivulets hurrying thro' the lawn,
The moan of doves in immemorial elms,
And murmuring of innumerable bees.

'Some men have written better poetry than I have' – Tennyson is supposed to
have said – 'but nobody has written poetry that sounds better.' This lyrical
piece from The Princess bears out that claim as well as any of his works. It
should be read aloud for full effect – but then, so should most poetry.

A Wish

SAMUEL ROGERS

Mine be a cot beside the hill;
    A bee-hive's hum shall soothe my ear;
A willowy brook, that turns a mill,
    With many a fall, shall linger near.

The swallow oft beneath my thatch
    Shall twitter from her clay-built nest;
Oft shall the pilgrim lift the latch
    And share my meal, a welcome guest.

Around my ivied porch shall spring
    Each fragrant flower that drinks the dew;
And Lucy at her wheel shall sing
    In russet gown and apron blue.

The village church among the trees,
    Where first our marriage vows were giv'n,
With merry peals shall swell the breeze
    And point with taper spire to Heav'n.

A hankering after a simple, quiet, countrified existence can be found somewhere in most people and keeps coming up in poetry, as here. The fact that Rogers, a wealthy man, enjoyed London society far too much ever to give it up says nothing about his sincerity or lack of it. He is expressing not an intention but, as he says, a wish.

Phillada Flouts Me

ANONYMOUS

O What a plague is love!
    How shall I bear it?
She will inconstant prove,
    I greatly fear it.
She so torments my mind
    That my strength faileth,
And wavers with the wind
    As a ship saileth.
Please her the best I may,
She loves still to gainsay;
Alack and well-a-day!
    Phillada flouts me.

At the fair yesterday
    She did pass by me;
She look'd another way
    And would not spy me:
I woo'd her for to dine,
    But could not get her;
Will had her to the wine –
    He might entreat her.
With Daniel she did dance,
On me she look'd askance;
O thrice unhappy chance!
    Phillada flouts me.

Fair maiden, have a care,
    And in time take me;
I can have those as fair
    If you forsake me:
For Doll, the dairy-maid
    Laugh'd at me lately,
And wanton Winifred
    Favours me greatly,
One throws milk on my clothes,
T'other plays with my nose;
What wanting signs are those?
    Phillada flouts me.

I cannot work nor sleep
    At all in season:
Love wounds my heart so deep
    Without all reason.
I 'gin to pine away
    In my love's shadow,
Like as a fat beast may,
    Penn'd in a meadow.
I shall be dead, I fear,
    Within this thousand year:
And all for that my dear
    Phillada flouts me.

The song of the disappointed lover, complaining that the object of his affection treats him with indifference or cruelty, was thick on the ground for centuries. What lifts this one out of the ruck, for me, is the sense that the fellow finds himself slightly ridiculous and the moment of resignation at the end.

Mental Cases 82

WILFRED OWEN

Who are these? Why sit they here in twilight?
Wherefore rock they, purgatorial shadows,
Drooping tongues from jaws that slob their relish,
Baring teeth that leer like skulls' teeth wicked?
Stroke on stroke of pain, – but what slow panic,
Gouged these chasms round their fretted sockets?
Ever from their hair and through their hands' palms
Misery swelters. Surely we have perished
Sleeping, and walk hell; but who these hellish?

– These are men whose minds the Dead have ravished.
Memory fingers in their hair of murders,
Multitudinous murders they once witnessed.
Wading sloughs of flesh these helpless wander,
Treading blood from lungs that had loved laughter.
Always they must see these things and hear them,
Batter of guns and shatter of flying muscles,
Carnage incomparable, and human squander,
Rucked too thick for these men's extrication.

[continued]

Therefore still their eyeballs shrink tormented
Back into their brains, because on their sense
Sunlight seems a blood-smear; night comes blood-black;
Dawn breaks open like a wound that bleeds afresh.
– Thus their heads wear this hilarious, hideous,
Awful falseness of set-smiling corpses.
– Thus their hands are plucking at each other;
Picking at the rope-knots of their scourging;
Snatching after us who smote them, brother,
Pawing us who dealt them war and madness.

Owen might have become the greatest English poet of our century if he had not been killed on the Western front a week before the 1918 Armistice, aged 25, the same age as Keats when he died. 'My subject is War, and the pity of War,' Owen wrote. He never made it seem more pitiful than in this poem about a military mental hospital.

83

Hail, Holy Light

JOHN MILTON

Hail, holy Light, offspring of Heaven first-born,
Or of the Eternal coeternal beam
May I express thee unblamed? since God is light,
And never but in unapproached light
Dwelt from eternity, dwelt then in thee,
Bright effluence of bright essence increate.
Or hear'st thou rather pure ethereal stream,
Whose fountain who shall tell? Before the Sun,
Before the Heavens thou wert, and at the voice
Of God, as with a mantle didst invest
The rising world of waters dark and deep,
Won from the void and formless infinite.
Thee I revisit now with bolder wing,
Escaped the Stygian pool, though long detained
In that obscure sojourn, while in my flight
Through utter and through middle darkness borne
With other notes than to the Orphean lyre
I sung of Chaos and eternal Night,
Taught by the Heavenly Muse to venture down
The dark descent, and up to reascend,
Though hard and rare. Thee I revisit safe,

And feel thy sovran vital lamp; but thou
Revisit'st not these eyes, that roll in vain
To find thy piercing ray, and find no dawn;
So thick a drop serene hath quenched their orbs.
Or dim suffusion veiled . . .
            Thus with the year
Seasons return; but not to me returns
Day, or the sweet approach of even or morn,
Or sight of vernal bloom, or summer's rose,
Or flocks, or herds, or human face divine;
But cloud instead, and ever-during dark
Surrounds me, from the cheerful ways of men
Cut off, and for the book of knowledge fair
Presented with a universal blank
Of Nature's works to me expunged and rased,
And wisdom at one entrance quite shut out.
So much the rather thou, celestial Light,
Shine inward, and the mind through all her powers
Irradiate, there plant eyes, all mist from thence
Purge and disperse, that I may see and tell
Of things invisible to mortal sight.

In this celebrated extract from his epic poem Paradise Lost, *Milton is addressing more than one kind of light. At the start, Light is a spiritual or divine force, perhaps the Son of God. Later, sunlight is meant, lost to Milton when he became totally blind some years earlier. The 'drop serene' is a medical term for the form of blindness he suffered from.*

84 *So, We'll Go No More A-Roving*

GEORGE GORDON, LORD BYRON

So, we'll go no more a-roving
  So late into the night,
Though the heart be still as loving,
  And the moon be still as bright.

For the sword outwears its sheath,
  And the soul wears out the breast,
And the heart must pause to breathe,
  And love itself have rest.

Though the night was made for loving,
  And the day returns too soon,
Yet we'll go no more a-roving
  By the light of the moon.

*Byron wrote a number of long poems and a few short lyrics like this one.
Everything is handled so gracefully and confidently that we forget to wonder
exactly what is being said, and never mind that he himself showed no signs of
stopping going a-roving in any sense. The way the last line catches its breath is
a masterstroke.*

From Greenland's Icy Mountains 85

REGINALD HEBER

From Greenland's icy mountains,
From India's coral strand,
Where Afric's sunny fountains
Roll down their golden sand,
From many an ancient river,
From many a palmy plain,
They call us to deliver
Their land from error's chain.

What though the spicy breezes
Blow soft o'er Java's isle,
Though every prospect pleases
And only man is vile,
In vain with lavish kindness
The gifts of God are strown,
The heathen in his blindness
Bows down to wood and stone.

Can we, whose souls are lighted
With wisdom from on high,
Can we to men benighted
The lamp of life deny?
Salvation! oh, salvation!
The joyful sound proclaim,
Till each remotest nation
Has learned Messiah's name.

Waft, waft, ye winds, his story,
And you, ye waters, roll,
Till, like a sea of glory,
It spreads from pole to pole;
Till o'er our ransomed nature
The Lamb for sinners slain,
Redeemer, King, Creator,
In bliss returns to reign.

Heber was another churchman, becoming Bishop of Calcutta in 1823. Hard
work in the trying climate hastened his death. He wrote a number of hymns of
which this was one of the most popular. Written when the Church still had no
doubts about its mission to convert the 'heathen' everywhere, it has dated in its
attitudes but remains a splendid poem.

A Garden by the Sea

WILLIAM MORRIS

I know a little garden-close,
Set thick with lily and red rose,
Where I would wander if I might
From dewy dawn to dewy night,
And have one with me wandering.

And though within it no birds sing,
And though no pillared house is there,
And though the apple-boughs are bare
Of fruit and blossom, would to God
Her feet upon the green grass trod,
And I beheld them as before.

There comes a murmer from the shore,
And in the place two fair streams are,
Drawn from the purple hills afar,
Drawn down unto the restless sea:
Dark hills whose heath-bloom feeds no bee,
Dark shore no ship has ever seen,
Tormented by the billows green
Whose murmur comes unceasingly
Unto the place for which I cry.

For which I cry both day and night,
For which I let slip all delight,
Whereby I grow both deaf and blind,
Careless to win, unskilled to find,
And quick to lose what all men seek.
Yet tottering as I am and weak,
Still have I left a little breath
To seek within the jaws of death
An entrance to that happy place,
To seek the unforgotten face,
Once seen, once kissed, once reft from me
Anigh the murmuring the sea.

As well as a poet, Morris was a painter, an interior decorator, a tapestry-
maker, a printer and an active socialist. Even in the Victorian era he was
outstanding for his energy. His poetry is generally rather thin in human interest
but once or twice, as here, personal feeling manages to break through.

The Burial of Sir John Moore at Corunna

CHARLES WOLFE

Not a drum was heard, not a funeral note,
  As his corse to the rampart we hurried;
Not a soldier discharged his farewell shot
  O'er the grave where our hero we buried.

We buried him darkly at dead of night,
  The sods with our bayonets turning,
By the struggling moonbeam's misty light
  And the lanthorn dimly burning.

No useless coffin enclosed his breast,
  Not in sheet nor in shroud we wound him;
But he lay like a warrior taking his rest
  With his martial cloak around him.

Few and short were the prayers we said,
  And we spoke not a word of sorrow;
But we steadfastly gazed on the face that was dead,
  And we bitterly thought of the morrow.

We thought as we hollowed his narrow bed
  And smoothed down his lonely pillow,
That the foe and the stranger would tread o'er his head,
  And we far away on the billow.

Lightly they'll talk of the spirit that's gone,
  And o'er his cold ashes upbraid him –
But little he'll reck, if they let him sleep on
  In the grave where a Briton has laid him.

But half of our heavy task was done
  When the clock struck the hour for retiring;
And we heard the distant and random gun
  That the foe was sullenly firing.

Slowly and sadly we laid him down;
  From the field of his fame fresh and gory.
We carved not a line, and we raised not a stone,
  But we left him alone with his glory.

There are few poets who are remembered for just one poem. Charles Wolfe is a prime example. He was a clergyman, dead at the age of 31. He is supposed to have written this stirring poem, describing an incident in the Peninsular War, at a single sitting.

Ha'nacker Mill

HILAIRE BELLOC

Sally is gone that was so kindly
Sally is gone from Ha'nacker Hill,
And the Briar grows ever since then so blindly
And ever since then the clapper is still,
And the sweeps have fallen from Ha'nacker Mill.

Ha'nacker Hill is in Desolation:
Ruin a-top and a field unploughed.
And Spirits that call on a fallen nation
Spirits that loved her calling aloud:
Spirits abroad in a windy cloud.

Spirits that call and no one answers;
Ha'nacker's down and England's done.
Wind and Thistle for pipe and dancers
And never a ploughman under the Sun.
Never a ploughman. Never a one.

Joseph Hilaire Pierre Belloc was the son of a French barrister but brought up in
England. He is remembered today not for his bombastic political writings but
for his light verse. Just occasionally, too, he brings off a serious poem that goes
with a swing all its own, as in this lament, for the passing of the old rural
England.

Drinking Song

89

ANONYMOUS

She tells me with claret she cannot agree,
And she thinks of a hogshead whene'er she sees me;
For I smell like a beast and therefore must I
Resolve to forsake her, or claret deny.
Must I leave my dear bottle, that was always my friend,
And I hope will continue so to my life's end?
Must I leave it for her? 'Tis a very hard task:
Let her go to the devil! – bring the other full flask.

Had she taxed me with gaming, and bid me forbear,
'Tis a thousand to one I had lent her an ear:
Had she found out my Sally, up three pair of stairs,
I had balked her, and gone to St. James's to prayers.
Had she bade me read homilies three times a day,
She perhaps had been humoured with little to say;
But, at night, to deny me my bottle of red,
Let her go to the devil! – there's no more to be said.

*Drinking songs in English go back to the Middle Ages and maybe further. Some
are probably quite good fun when bawled to music with a glass in the hand, but
they look pretty flat on the printed page. This poem, however, is something
different – a pen-portrait of a soak that is not at all funny.*

Abide with Me

HENRY FRANCIS LYTE

Abide with me; fast falls the eventide;
The darkness deepens; Lord, with me abide.
When other helpers fail, and comforts flee.
Help of the helpless, O abide with me!

Swift to its close ebbs out life's little day;
Earth's joys grow dim, its glories pass away:
Change and decay in all around I see,
O Thou who changest not, abide with me.

Not a brief glance I beg, a passing word;
But as Thou dweltst with Thy disciples, Lord,
Familiar, condescending, patient, free,
Come, not to sojourn, but abide with me.

Come not in terrors, as the King of kings;
But kind and good, with healing in Thy wings,
Tears for all woes, a heart for every plea,
Come, Friend of sinners, and thus bide with me.

Thou on my head in early youth didst smile,
And, though rebellious and perverse meanwhile,
Thou hast not left me, oft as I left Thee,
On to the close, O Lord, abide with me!

I need Thy presence every passing hour;
What but Thy grace can foil the tempter's power?
Who like Thyself my guide and stay can be?
Through cloud and sunshine, Lord, abide with me.

I fear no foe with Thee at hand to bless;
Ills have no weight and tears no bitterness;
Where is death's sting? Where, grave, Thy victory?
I triumph still if Thou abide with me.

Hold Thou Thy cross before my closing eyes;
Shine through the gloom and point me to the skies!
Heaven's morning breaks and earth's vain shadows flee:
In life, in death, O Lord, abide with me.

This famous hymn, like many others of its kind, is a striking religious poem in its own right. In fact, seen and read in the full version, as here, rather than sung in a cut one, it reveals what a passionate and personal cry it is.

Executive

SIR JOHN BETJEMAN

I am a young executive. No cuffs than mine are cleaner;
I have a Slimline brief-case and I use the firm's Cortina.
In every roadside hostelry from here to Burgess Hill
The maîtres d'hôtel all know me well and let me sign the bill.

You ask me what it is I do. Well actually, you know,
I'm partly a liaison man and partly P.R.O.
Essentially I integrate the current export drive
And basically I'm viable from ten o'clock till five.

For vital off-the-record work – that's talking transport-wise –
I've a scarlet Aston-Martin – and does she go? She flies!
Pedestrians and dogs and cats – we mark them down for slaughter.
I also own a speed-boat which has never touched the water.

She's built of fibre-glass, of course, I call her 'Mandy Jane'
After a bird I used to know – No soda, please, just plain –
And how did I acquire her? Well to tell you about that
And to put you in the picture I must wear my other hat.

I do some mild developing. The sort of place I need
Is a quiet country market town that's rather run to seed.
A luncheon and a drink or two, a little savoir faire –
I fix the Planning Officer, the Town Clerk and the Mayor.

And if some preservationist attempts to interfere
A 'dangerous structure' notice from the Borough Engineer
Will settle any buildings that are standing in our way –
The modern style, sir, with respect, has really come to stay.

Here, we see Sir John Betjeman at his wonderfully comic and observant best.

My Lord Tomnoddy

ROBERT BROUGH

My Lord Tomnoddy's the son of an Earl,
His hair is straight, but his whiskers curl;
His Lordship's forehead is far from wide,
But there's plenty of room for the brains inside.
He writes his name with indifferent ease,
He's rather uncertain about the 'd' s, –
But what does it matter, if three or one,
To the Earl of Fitzdotterel's eldest son?

My Lord Tomnoddy to college went,
Much time he lost, much money he spent;
Rules, and windows and heads, he broke –
Authorities winked – young men will joke!
He never peeped inside of a book –
In two years' time a degree he took;
And the newspapers vaunted the honours won
By the Earl of Fitzdotterel's eldest son.

. . . . . .

My Lord Tomnoddy must settle down –
There's a vacant seat in the family town!
('Tis time he should sow his eccentric oats) –
He hasn't the wit to apply for votes:
He cannot e'en learn his election speech,
Three phrases he speaks – a mistake in each!
And then breaks down – but the borough is won
For the Earl of Fitzdotterel's eldest son.

My Lord Tomnoddy prefers the Guards,
(The House is a bore) so! – it's on the cards!
My Lord's a Lieutenant at twenty-three,
A Captain at twenty-six is he –
He never drew sword, except on drill;
The tricks of parade he has learnt but ill –
A full-blown Colonel at thirty-one
Is the Earl of Fitzdotterel's eldest son!

My Lord Tomnoddy is thirty-four;
The Earl can last but a few years more.
My Lord in the Peers will take his place:
Her Majesty's councils his words will grace.
Office he'll hold, and patronage sway;
Fortunes and lives he will vote away –
And what are his qualifications? – ONE!
He's the Earl of Fitzdotterel's eldest son.

*Anything that might be called 'protest' verse was rare before the present
century. This exception is taken from Songs of the Governing Classes,
published in 1855, a volume of satirical poems attacking hereditary power and
excessive wealth. Brough, journalist and playwright as well as poet, is an
obscure figure today.*

Song   93

CHRISTINA ROSSETTI

When I am dead, my dearest,
    Sing no sad songs for me;
Plant thou no roses at my head,
    Nor shady cypress tree:
Be the green grass above me
    With showers and dewdrops wet;
And if thou wilt, remember,
    And if thou wilt, forget.

I shall not see the shadows,
    I shall not feel the rain;
I shall not hear the nightingale
    Sing on, as if in pain;
And dreaming through the twilight
    That doth not rise nor set,
Haply I may remember,
    And haply may forget.

*We have already included Christina's sonnet, 'Remember' (No. 50). In this
poem, written this previous year, she treats the same theme – remembrance
and forgetfulness after her death – in a lyrical way. As often happens, the 'tune'
of the poem seems to run against the sense of the words.*

Lead, Kindly Light

JOHN HENRY NEWMAN

Lead, kindly Light, amid the encircling gloom,
    Lead thou me on;
The night is dark, and I am far from home,
    Lead Thou me on.
Keep Thou my feet; I do not ask to see
The distant scene; one step enough for me.

I was not ever thus, nor prayed that Thou
    Should'st lead me on;
I loved to choose and see my path; but now
    Lead Thou me on.
I loved the garish day, and, spite of fears,
Pride ruled my will: remember not past years.

So long Thy power hath blest me, sure it still
    Will lead me on,
O'er moor and fen, o'er crag and torrent, till
    The night is gone,
And with the morn those angel faces smile,
Which I have loved long since, and lost awhile.

*Newman was an Anglican clergyman who later become a Roman Catholic and,
in old age, a cardinal of that Church. He wrote a great deal on church matters
and was a celebrated Victorian public figure, but there is nothing public or
grand about this example of his religious poetry, a humble personal prayer,
once a famous hymn.*

O Swallow, Swallow

ALFRED, LORD TENNYSON

O Swallow, Swallow, flying, flying South,
Fly to her, and fall upon her gilded eaves,
And tell her, tell her, what I tell to thee.

O tell her, Swallow, thou that knowest each,
That bright and fierce and fickle is the South,
And dark and true and tender is the North.

O Swallow, Swallow, if I could follow, and light
Upon her lattice, I would pipe and trill,
And cheep and twitter twenty million loves.

O were I thou that she might take me in,
And lay me on her bosom, and her heart
Would rock the snowy cradle till I died.

Why lingereth she to clothe her heart with love,
Delaying as the tender ash delays
To clothe herself, when all the woods are green?

O tell her, Swallow, that thy brood is flown:
Say to her, I do but wanton in the South,
But in the North long since my nest is made.

O tell her, brief is life but love is long,
And brief the sun of summer in the North,
And brief the moon of beauty in the South.

O Swallow, flying from the golden woods,
Fly to her, and pipe and woo her, and make her mine,
And tell her, tell her, that I follow thee.

*Although he wrote a lot of narrative verse, Tennyson's genius was for something
more reflective or emotional than a story. The body of his long poem The
Princess is largely forgotten today, but the occasional songs in it are very
much alive. He wrote this one first in rhyme and then, for some reason, rewrote
it in its present form.*

96 She Was a Phantom of Delight

WILLIAM WORDSWORTH

She was a phantom of delight
When first she gleam'd upon my sight;
A lovely apparition sent
To be a moment's ornament;
Her eyes as stars of twilight fair;
Like twilight's, too, her dusky hair;
But all things else about her drawn
From May-time and the cheerful dawn;
A dancing shape, an image gay,
To haunt, to startle, and waylay.

I saw her upon nearer view,
A Spirit, yet a Woman too!
Her household motions light and free,
And steps of virgin liberty:
A countenance in which did meet
Sweet records, promises as sweet;
A creature not too bright or good
For human nature's daily food;
For transient sorrows, simple wiles,
Praise, blame, love, kisses, tears, and smiles.

And now I see with eye serene
The very pulse of the machine;
A being breathing thoughtful breath,
A traveller betwixt life and death:
The reason firm, the temperate will,
Endurance, foresight, strength, and skill;
A perfect Woman, nobly plann'd,
To warn, to comfort, and command;
And yet a Spirit still, and bright
With something of angelic light.

The people in Wordsworth's poems often seem to interest him more as abstract
symbols or types than as individuals. There is something of that here, with the
character standing for Woman as well as being an actual woman. But he
makes her real enough and conveys clearly her progress from girlhood to
maturity.

Newark Abbey

THOMAS LOVE PEACOCK

I gaze where August's sunbeam falls
Along these gray and lonely walls,
Till in its light absorbed appears
The lapse of five-and-thirty years.
    If change there be, I trace it not
In all this consecrated spot:
No new imprint of Ruin's march
On roofless wall and frameless arch:
The woods, the hills, the fields, the stream,
Are basking in the self-same beam:
The fall, that turns the unseen mill,
As then it murmured, murmurs still.
It seems as if in one were cast
The present and the imaged past;
Spanning, as with a bridge sublime,
That awful lapse of human time;
That gulf, unfathomably spread
Between the living and the dead.

    For all too well my spirit feels
The only change this scene reveals.
The sunbeams play, the breezes stir,
Unseen, unfelt, unheard by her,
Who, on that long-past August day,
Beheld with me these ruins gray.

    Whatever span the fates allow,
Ere I shall be as she is now,
Still, in my bosom's inmost cell,
Shall that deep-treasured memory dwell;
That, more than language can express,
Pure miracle of loveliness,
Whose voice so sweet, whose eyes so bright,
Were my soul's music, and its light,
In those blest days when life was new,
And hope was false, but love was true.

Peacock's fame rests on his entertaining satirical novels, which contain some lively songs. His more serious poems are mostly less successful, but he did produce this touching memorial to an early love of his who died young. He had visited the ruins of Newark Abbey, Ripley, Surrey, with her in 1807 and returned there alone in 1842.

98 Jerusalem, My Happy Home

ANONYMOUS

Jerusalem, my happy home,
　　When shall I come to thee?
When shall my sorrows have an end?
　　Thy joys when shall I see?

O happy harbour of the saints,
　　O sweet and pleasant soil!
In thee no sorrow may be found,
　　No grief, no care, no toil.

No dampish mist is seen in thee,
　　Nor cold nor darksome night;
There every soul shines as the sun,
　　There God himself gives light.

There lust and lucre cannot dwell,
　　There envy bears no sway;
There is no hunger, heat nor cold,
　　But pleasure every way.

　　　·　·　·　·　·　·

Thy houses are of ivory,
　　Thy windows crystal clear,
Thy tiles are made of beaten gold,
　　O God, that I were there.

Within thy gates doth nothing come
　　That is not passing clean;
No spider's web, no dirt, no dust,
　　No filth may there be seen.

　　　·　·　·　·　·　·

Thy gardens and thy gallant walks
　　Continually are green;
There grows such sweet and pleasant flowers
　　As nowhere else are seen.

　　　·　·　·　·　·　·

Jerusalem, my happy home,
   Would God I were in thee!
Would God my woes were at an end,
   Thy joys that I might see!

*This vision of Heaven comes unmistakably from the people. God himself is
there, of course, and the saints, and much beauty, but it is hardly less
important that work is finished for ever, that cold, hunger and discomfort are
no more. Whoever wrote the third verse knew all about getting up on dark
winter mornings to go to work in the fields.*

Ode 99

ARTHUR O'SHAUGHNESSY

We are the music makers,
   And we are the dreamers of dreams,
Wandering by lone sea-breakers,
   And sitting by desolate streams; –
World-losers and world-forsakers,
   On whom the pale moon gleams:
Yet we are the movers and shakers
   Of the world for ever, it seems.

    . . . . . .

A breath of our inspiration
Is the life of each generation;
   A wondrous thing of our dreaming
   Unearthly, impossible seeming –
The soldier, the king, and the peasant
   Are working together in one,
Till our dream shall become their present,
   And their work in the world be done.

    . . . . . .

[continued]

And therefore today is thrilling
With a past day's late fulfilling;
   And the multitudes are enlisted
   In the faith that their fathers resisted,
And, scorning the dream of tomorrow,
   Are bringing to pass, as they may,
In the world, for its joy or its sorrow,
   The dream that was scorned yesterday.

. . . .

Great hail! we cry to the comers
   From the dazzling unknown shore;
Bring us hither your sun and summers,
   And renew our world as of yore:
You shall teach us your song's new numbers,
   And things that we dreamed not before:
Yea, in spite of a dreamer who slumbers,
   And a singer who sings no more.

O'Shaughnessy is another single-poem poet, remembered for only one out of
the many he wrote. In the style of those days he combined a dreamy sort of
interest in the past with another, almost as dreamy perhaps, in some kind of
Utopian future. As a contemporary of his wrote, he had 'a haunting music all
of his own'.

Believe Me, If All Those Endearing Young Charms

100

THOMAS MOORE

Believe me, if all those endearing young charms,
    Which I gaze on so fondly to-day,
Were to change by to-morrow, and fleet in my arms,
    Like fairy-gifts, fading away!
Thou wouldst still be ador'd, as this moment thou art,
    Let thy loveliness fade as it will,
And, around the dear ruin, each wish of my heart
    Would entwine itself verdantly still!

It is not, while beauty and youth are thine own,
    And thy cheeks unprofan'd by a tear,
That the fervour and faith of a soul can be known,
    To which time will but make thee more dear!
No, the heart that has truly lov'd, never forgets,
    But as truly loves on to the close,
As the sun-flower turns on her god, when he sets,
    The same look which she turn'd when he rose!

Moore was the son of a Dublin grocer, a song-writer and commercially one of
the most successful poets of the last century. Until quite recently this piece was
very well known in its musical form. Some modern readers will find it touching
in a pleasant, unsensational way; to others it may seem over-sentimentalised.

Bredon Hill

A. E. HOUSMAN

In summertime on Bredon
    The bells they sound so clear;
Round both the shires they ring them
    In steeples far and near,
    A happy noise to hear.

Here of a Sunday morning
    My love and I would lie,
And see the coloured counties,
    And hear the larks so high
    About us in the sky.

The bells would ring to call her
    In valleys miles away:
'Come all to church, good people;
    Good people, come and pray.'
    But here my love would stay.

And I would turn and answer
    Among the springing thyme,
'Oh, peal upon our wedding,
    And we will hear the chime,
    And come to church in time.'

But when the snows at Christmas
    On Bredon top were strown,
My love rose up so early
    And stole out unbeknown
    And went to church alone.

They tolled the one bell only,
    Groom there was none to see,
The mourners followed after,
    And so to church went she,
    And would not wait for me.

The bells they sound on Bredon,
And still the steeples hum.
'Come all to church, good people,' –
Oh, noisy bells, be dumb;
I hear you, I will come.

Alfred Edward Housman was a dried-up Cambridge don who was also a
marvellously gloomy poet. Human loss, the untimely death of a loved one, was
a favourite theme of his, as in this poem, which as usual with him is not based
on any incident in his own life. Bredon (pronounced Breedon, he says in a note)
is in what was then Worcestershire.

The Marriage of True Minds   102

WILLIAM SHAKESPEARE

Let me not to the marriage of true minds
Admit impediments. Love is not love
Which alters when it alteration finds,
Or bends with the remover to remove.
O, No! It is an ever-fixed mark,
That looks on tempests and is never shaken;
It is the star to every wandering bark,
Whose worth's unknown, although his height be taken.
Love's not Time's fool, though rosy lips and cheeks
Within his bending sickle's compass come;
Love alters not with his brief hours and weeks,
But bears it out even to the edge of doom.
　　If this be error, and upon me prov'd,
　　I never writ, nor no man ever lov'd.

Shakespeare's sonnets are probably admired more than they are read, and it is
no use pretending they are easy to understand. But anyone with a taste for
poetry is likely to respond to their music while perhaps missing some of the
meaning. Fortunately this famous one is clear enough in its outline, at least.

103 # The Hill Farmer Speaks

R. S. THOMAS

I am the farmer, stripped of love
And thought and grace by the land's hardness;
But what I am saying over the fields'
Desolate acres, rough with dew,
Is, Listen, listen, I am a man like you.

The wind goes over the hill pastures
Year after year, and the ewes starve,
Milkless, for want of the new grass.
And I starve, too, for something the spring
Can never foster in veins run dry.

The pig is a friend, the cattle's breath
Mingles with mine in the still lanes;
I wear it willingly like a cloak
To shelter me from your curious gaze.

The hens go in and out at the door
From sun to shadow, as stray thoughts pass
Over the floor of my wide skull.
The dirt is under my cracked nails;
The tale of my life is smirched with dung;
The phlegm rattles. But what I am saying
Over the grasses rough with dew
Is, Listen, listen, I am a man like you.

For many years Ronald Stuart Thomas was a country rector of the Anglican
Church in Wales. Although he has written a great deal about life in the Welsh
hill country his work makes a direct appeal to many who have never been to
Wales. His view of the people and the countryside is not a soft or
sentimental one.

Assault Convoy

NORMAN HAMPSON

How quietly they push the flat sea from them,
Shadows against the night, that grow to meet us
And fade back slowly to our zig-zag rhythm –
The silent pattern dim destroyers weave.
The first light greets them friendly; pasteboard ships
Erect in lineless mists of sky and sea.
A low sun lingers on the well-known outlines
That take new beauty from this sombre war-paint;
Familiar names trail childish memories
Of peace-time ports and waving, gay departures.

Only at intervals the truth breaks on us
Like catspaws, ruffling these quiet waters.
Our future is unreal, a thing to read of
Later; a chapter in a history book.
We cannot see the beaches where the dead
Must fall before this waxing moon is full;
The tracer-vaulted sky, the gun's confusion,
Searchlights and shouted orders, sweating fumbling
As landing craft are lowered; the holocaust
Grenade and bayonet will build upon these beaches.

We are dead, numbed, atrophied, sunk in the swamps of war.
Each of those thousands is a life entire.
No skilful simile can hide their sheer humanity.
Across the narrowing seas our enemies wait,
Each man the centre of his darkening world;
Bound, as we are, by humanity's traces of sorrow
To anxious women, alone in the menacing night,
Where the rhythm of Europe is lost in their private fear
And El Dorado cannot staunch their grief.

This poem perfectly captures the feeling of the tension as seaborne troops move
in towards an enemy-held coast. Norman Hampson served in the navy during
the war and spent two years as a liaison officer to the Free French Forces. He
teaches now at York University. (El Dorado is a legendary city of infinite
wealth.)

105

Renouncement

ALICE MEYNELL

I must not think of thee; and, tired yet strong,
　I shun the thought that lurks in all delight –
　The thought of thee – and in the blue Heaven's height,
And in the dearest passage of a song.

Oh, just beyond the fairest thoughts that throng
　This breast, the thought of thee waits hidden, yet bright;
　But it must never, never come in sight;
I must stop short of thee the whole day long.

But when sleep comes to close each difficult day,
　When night gives pause to the long watch I keep,
　And all my bonds I needs must loose apart,
Must doff my will as raiment laid away, –
　With the first dream that comes with the first sleep
　I run, I run, I am gathered to thy heart.

*This sonnet, for which its author is nowadays chiefly remembered, achieved
instant fame when it was first published in the 1870s. Evidently Dante Gabriel
Rossetti went round reciting it by heart to his friends, and Browning was quite
bowled over. Even today it does sound very much like something based on
personal experience.*

Rule, Britannia

JAMES THOMSON

When Britain first, at heaven's command,
  Arose from out the azure main;
This was the charter of the land,
  And guardian Angels sung this strain:
    'Rule, Britannia, rule the waves;
    Britons never will be slaves.'

The nations not so blest as thee,
  Must, in their turns, to tyrants fall:
While thou shalt flourish great and free,
  The dread and envy of them all.
    'Rule, etc.

Still more majestic shalt thou rise,
  More dreadful, from each foreign stroke:
As the loud blast that tears the skies,
  Serves but to root thy native oak.
    'Rule, etc.

Thee haughty tyrants ne'er shall tame:
  All their attempts to bend thee down,
Will but arouse thy generous flame;
  But work their woe, and thy renown.
    'Rule, etc.

To thee belongs the rural reign;
  Thy cities shall with commerce shine:
All thine shall be the subject main,
  And every shore it circles thine.
    'Rule, etc.

The Muses, still with freedom found,
  Shall to thy happy coast repair:
Blest isle! with matchless beauty crown'd,
  And many hearts to guard the fair.
    'Rule, Britannia, rule the waves;
    Britons never will be slaves.'

How many of the millions who have sung these words could name their author?
Thomson was a Scot who wrote nature poems, boring verse plays and a
masque, or music-poetry-singing-dancing entertainment, that included this.
Notice that he wrote not 'rules the waves' (boasting) but 'rule the waves'
(serious advice).

To Sleep

107

JOHN KEATS

O soft embalmer of the still midnight,
  Shutting, with careful fingers and benign,
Our gloom-pleased eyes, embowered from the light,
  Enshaded in forgetfulness divine:
O soothest Sleep! If so it please thee, close,
  In midst of this thine hymn, my willing eyes,
Or wait the 'Amen', ere thy poppy throws
  Around my bed its lulling charities.
Then save me, or the passed day will shine
Upon my pillow, breeding many woes;
  Save me from curious conscience, that still hoards
Its strength for darkness, burrowing like a mole;
  Turn the key deftly in the oiled wards,
And seal the hushed casket of my soul.

*Most of Keats's best poems were, like this one, written in the two years before
his early death from consumption. He was always interested in poetic forms
and this sonnet is to some degree an experiment. The rhyme-scheme is an
invention of his, aimed at avoiding a final couplet.*

Elegy for Himself

CHIDIOCK TICHBORNE

My prime of youth is but a frost of cares,
　My feast of joy is but a dish of pain,
My crop of corn is but a field of tares,
　　And all my good is but vain hope of gain;
　　　The day is past, and yet I saw no sun,
　　　And now I live, and now my life is done.

My tale was heard and yet it was not told,
　My fruit is fallen and yet my leaves are green,
My youth is spent and yet I am not old,
　　I saw the world and yet I was not seen;
　　　My thread is cut and yet it is not spun,
　　　And now I live, and now my life is done.

I sought my death and found it in my womb,
　I looked for life and saw it was a shade,
I trod the earth and knew it was my tomb,
　　And now I die, and now I was but made;
　　　My glass is full, and now my glass is run,
　　　And now I live, and now my life is done.

*This extraordinary poem has been a favourite with successive generations.
There seems no reason to doubt the tradition that Tichborne wrote it in the
Tower of London on the night before his execution for treason. By a grim irony
it was first published in the year of his death in a volume called* Verses of
Praise and Joy.

109 # The Graves of a Household

FELICIA DOROTHEA HEMANS

They grew in beauty side by side,
    They filled one home with glee; –
Their graves are scattered far and wide,
    By mount, and stream, and sea.

The same fond mother bent at night
    O'er each fair sleeping brow:
She had each folded flower in sight –
    Where are those dreamers now?

One, 'midst the forest of the West,
    By a dark stream is laid –
The Indian knows his place of rest,
    Far in the cedar shade.

The sea, the blue lone sea, hath one –
    He lies where pearls lie deep,
He was the loved of all, yet none
    O'er his low bed may weep.

One sleeps where southern vines are drest
    Above the noble slain:
He wrapt his colours round his breast
    On a blood-red field of Spain.

And one – o'er her the myrtle showers
    Its leaves, by soft winds fanned;
She faded 'midst Italian flowers –
    The last of that bright band.

And parted thus they rest, who played
    Beneath the same green tree;
Whose voices mingled as they prayed
    Around one parent knee!

They that with smiles lit up the hall,
    And cheered with song the hearth! –
Alas, for love! If thou wert all,
    And nought beyond, O Earth!

Mrs Hemans was a well-known poet in her day. It is interesting that a brother
of hers was a soldier who served in Spain during the Peninsular War. Though
he survived this, fears for his safety might have given his sister the idea for the
poem. And then again, of course, they might well not.

At Grass

PHILIP LARKIN

The eye can hardly pick them out
From the cold shade they shelter in,
Till wind distresses tail and mane;
Then one crops grass, and moves about
– The other seeming to look on –
And stands anonymous again.

Yet fifteen years ago, perhaps
Two dozen distances sufficed
To fable them: faint afternoons
Of Cups and Stakes and Handicaps,
Whereby their names were artificed
To inlay faded, classic Junes –

Silks at the start: against the sky
Numbers and parasols: outside,
Squadrons of empty cars, and heat,
And littered grass: then the long cry
Hanging unhushed till it subside
To stop-press columns on the street.

Do memories plague their ears like flies?
They shake their heads. Dusk brims the shadows.
Summer by summer all stole away,
The starting-gates, the crowds and cries –
All but the unmolesting meadows.
Almanacked, their names live; they

Have slipped their names, and stand at ease,
Or gallop for what must be joy,
And not a fieldglass sees them home,
Or curious stop-watch prophesies;
Only the groom, and the groom's boy,
With bridles in the evening come.

*Larkin's work is remarkable for the ease and naturalness with which he moves
from an ordinary incident or scene, in this case a pair of old racehorses grazing,
to deep considerations of human life. Everything is beautifully crafted.*

111 # The Owl and the Pussy-Cat

EDWARD LEAR

The Owl and the Pussy-Cat went to sea
   In a beautiful pea-green boat.
They took some honey, and plenty of money
   Wrapped up in a five-pound note.
The Owl looked up to the stars above,
   And sang to a small guitar,
'O lovely Pussy! O Pussy, my love,
   What a beautiful Pussy you are,
      You are,
      You are!
   What a beautiful Pussy you are!'

Pussy said to the Owl, 'You elegant fowl!
   How charmingly sweet you sing!
O let us be married! Too long we have tarried:
   But what shall we do for a ring?'
They sailed away, for a year and a day,
   To the land where the Bong-Tree grows,
And there in a wood a Piggy-wig stood,
   With a ring at the end of his nose,
      His nose,
      His nose!
   With a ring at the end of his nose.

'Dear Pig, are you willing to sell for one shilling
   Your ring?' Said the Piggy, 'I will.'
So they took it away, and were married next day
   By the Turkey who lives on the hill.
They dined on mince, and slices of quince,
   Which they ate with a runcible spoon;
And hand in hand, on the edge of the sand,
   They danced by the light of the moon,
      The moon,
      The moon,
   They danced by the light of the moon.

Lear was an eccentric, an illustrator and landscape painter, a great traveller by
Victorian standards and a writer of humorous or nonsense verse that won him a
cult following. Most of this verse is a bit whimsical, even twee to some tastes,
but in this poem and one or two others he hit a genuine note of fantasy and
romance.

The Patriot: An Old Story   112

ROBERT BROWNING

It was roses, roses, all the way,
    With myrtle mixed in my path like mad:
The house-roofs seemed to heave and sway,
    The church-spires flamed, such flags they had,
A year ago on this very day.

The air broke into a mist with bells,
    The old walls rocked with the crowd and cries.
Had I said, 'Good folk, mere noise repels –
    But give me your sun from yonder skies!'
They had answered, 'And afterward, what else?'

Alack, it was I who leaped at the sun,
    To give it my loving friends to keep!
Naught man could do, have I left undone:
    And you see my harvest, what I reap
This very day, now a year is run.

There's nobody on the house-tops now –
    Just a palsied few at the windows set;
For the best of the sight is, all allow,
    At the Shambles' Gate – or, better yet,
By the very scaffold's foot, I trow.

I go in the rain, and, more than needs,
    A rope cuts both my wrists behind;
And I think, by the feel, my forehead bleeds,
    For they fling, whoever has a mind,
Stones at me for my year's misdeeds.

Thus I entered, and thus I go!
    In triumphs, people have dropped down dead.
'Paid by the world, what dost thou owe
    Me?' God might question; now instead,
'Tis God shall repay: I am safer so.

*Along with his poetic gifts Browning had a nose for a dramatic situation, a
story, that we more often associate with writers of fiction (in prose). Into this
poem he compresses an account of a revolutionary leader, hailed in his day as a
'patriot', now pushed out in his turn and sent to the scaffold. There are
contemporary parallels.*

113 To Mistress Margaret Hussey

JOHN SKELTON

Merry Margaret,
 As midsummer flower,
Gentle as falcon
 Or hawk of the tower:
With solace and gladness,
Much mirth and no madness,
All good and no badness;
 So joyously,
 So maidenly,
 So womanly
 Her demeaning
 In everything,
 Far, far passing
 That I can indite,
 Or suffice to write
Of merry Margaret
 As midsummer flower,
Gentle as falcon
 Or hawk of the tower.
As patient and as still
And as full of good will
As fair Isaphill,
 Coriander,
 Sweet pomander,
 Good Cassander,
Steadfast of thought,
Well made, well wrought,
Far may be sought
Ere that ye can find
So courteous, so kind,
As merry Margaret,
 This midsummer flower,
Gentle as falcon
 Or hawk of the tower.

For more than a century after the death of Chaucer in 1400, English poetry was in a bad way (as it is again now). Skelton kept the flag flying, but he was an eccentric and a joker and his poems are never straightforward, though this one mostly is. Falcons and hawks are not usually thought of as gentle but these would be tamed birds.

O Captain! My Captain 114

WALT WHITMAN

O Captain! my Captain! our fearful trip is done,
The ship has weather'd every rack, the prize we sought is won,
The port is near, the bells I hear, the people all exulting,
While follow eyes the steady keel, the vessel grim and daring;
    But O heart! heart! heart!
        O the bleeding drops of red,
           Where on the deck my Captain lies,
           Fallen cold and dead.

O Captain! my Captain! rise up and hear the bells;
Rise up – for you the flag is flung – for you the bugle trills,
For you bouquets and ribbon'd wreaths – for you the shores a-crowding,
For you they call, the swaying mass, their eager faces turning;
    Here Captain! dear father!
        This arm beneath your head!
           It is some dream that on the deck,
           You've fallen cold and dead.

My Captain does not answer, his lips are pale and still,
My father does not feel my arm, he has no pulse nor will,
The ship is anchor'd safe and sound, its voyage closed and done,
From fearful trip the victor ship comes in with object won:
    Exult O shores, and ring O bells!
        But I with mournful tread,
           Walk the deck my Captain lies,
           Fallen cold and dead.

*Whitman, born in Long Island, New York, left school at 11 but read
enormously and for years wandered about America talking to everybody he met
and writing away. He was a fervent patriot. Much of his work seems thin and
eccentric now but he did produce this remarkable short poem, perhaps out of his
experience of the Civil War.*

Sun and Fun

JOHN BETJEMAN

I walked into the night-club in the morning;
    There was kummel on the handle of the door.
The ashtrays were unemptied.
The cleaning unattempted,
    And a squashed tomato sandwich on the floor.

I pulled aside the thick magenta curtains
    – So Regency, so Regency, my dear –
And a host of little spiders
Ran a race across the ciders
    To a box of baby 'pollies by the beer.

Oh sun upon the summer-going by-pass
    Where ev'rything is speeding to the sea,
And wonder beyond wonder
That here where lorries thunder
    The sun should ever percolate to me.

When Boris used to call in his Sedanca,
    When Teddy took me down to his estate
When my nose excited passion,
When my clothes were in the fashion,
    When my beaux were never cross if I was late,

There was sun enough for lazing upon beaches,
    There was fun enough for far into the night.
But I'm dying now and done for,
What on earth was all that fun for?
    For I'm old and ill and terrified and tight.

Sir John Betjeman showed in his poems a great capacity for imagining and re-creating the feelings of people quite different from himself. In this poem, subtitled 'Song of a Night-Club Proprietress', he sets out in few words a world very different from his – amusingly, yes, but with sympathy and compassion too.

<h1 style="text-align:center">If—</h1>

RUDYARD KIPLING

If you can keep your head when all about you
    Are losing theirs and blaming it on you,
If you can trust yourself when all men doubt you,
    But make allowance for their doubting too;
If you can wait and not be tired by waiting,
    Or being lied about, don't deal in lies,
Or being hated, don't give way to hating,
    And yet don't look too good, nor talk too wise:

If you can dream – and not make dreams your master;
    If you can think – and not make thoughts your aim;
If you can meet with Triumph and Disaster
    And treat those two impostors just the same;
If you can bear to hear the truth you've spoken
    Twisted by knaves to make a trap for fools,
Or watch the things you gave your life to, broken,
    And stoop and build 'em up with worn-out tools:

If you can make one heap of all your winnings
    And risk it on one turn of pitch-and-toss,
And lose, and start again at your beginnings
    And never breathe a word about your loss;
If you can force your heart and nerve and sinew
    To serve your turn long after they are gone,
And so hold on when there is nothing in you
    Except the Will which says to them: 'Hold on!'

If you can talk with crowds and keep your virtue,
    Or walk with Kings – nor lose the common touch,
If neither foes nor loving friends can hurt you,
    If all men count with you, but none too much;
If you can fill the unforgiving minute
    With sixty seconds' worth of distance run,
Yours is the Earth and everything that's in it,
    And – which is more – you'll be a Man, my son!

*You can still come across framed broadsheets of this poem hung on the wall in
bars and clubs. In its day it came about as near as any has ever done to being a
poem everyone knew and almost everyone could recite a few phrases from.
Kipling is supposed to have had George Washington in mind when he wrote it.*

London

WILLIAM BLAKE

I wander thro' each charter'd street,
Near where the charter'd Thames does flow.
And mark in every face I meet
Marks of weakness, marks of woe.

In every cry of every Man,
In every Infant's cry of fear;
In every voice, in every ban,
The mind-forg'd manacles I hear.

How the Chimney-sweeper's cry
Every black'ning Church appalls,
And the hapless Soldier's sigh,
Runs in blood down Palace walls.

But most thro' midnight streets I hear
How the youthful Harlot's curse
Blasts the new-born Infant's tear
And blights with plagues the Marriage hearse.

*Blake was an illustrator and engraver, an extraordinary poet of a mystical bent,
and slightly mad. He had vague revolutionary visions of a paradise of anarchy
with religious and sexual tinges. But he also had a sharp eye for the miserable
lot of the London poor in the Industrial Revolution, as we see here.*

An English Wood

ROBERT GRAVES

This valley wood is pledged
To the set shape of things,
And reasonably hedged:
Here are no harpies fledged,
No rocs may clap their wings,
Nor gryphons wave their stings.
Here, poised in quietude,
Calm elementals brood
On the set shape of things:
They fend away alarms
From this green wood.
Here nothing is that harms –
No bulls with lungs of brass,
No toothed or spiny grass,
No tree whose clutching arms
Drink blood when travellers pass,
No mount of glass;
No bardic tongues unfold
Satires or charms.
Only, the lawns are soft,
The tree-stems, grave and old;
Slow branches sway aloft,
The evening air comes cold,
The sunset scatters gold.
Small grasses toss and bend,
Small pathways idly tend
Towards no fearful end.

Although he lived in Majorca for many years and was greatly learned in the literature of other cultures, Graves always insisted that English poetry must remain English, proof against foreign influence (including American). This poem of his illustrates that, not only in its subject, but also in its approach.

119

Lust in Action

WILLIAM SHAKESPEARE

The expense of spirit in a waste of shame
Is lust in action; and till action, lust
Is perjur'd, murderous, bloody, full of blame,
Savage, extreme, rude, cruel, not to trust;
Enjoy'd no sooner, but despised straight;
Past reason hunted, and no sooner had,
Past reason hated, as a swallow'd bait,
On purpose laid to make the taker mad;
Mad in pursuit, and in possession so;
Had, having, and in quest to have, extreme;
A bliss in proof, – and prov'd, a very woe;
Before, a joy propos'd; behind, a dream:
    All this the world well knows; yet none knows well
    To shun the heaven that leads men to this hell.

As his plays show, Shakespeare knew all about the darker side of human nature. He was also a very observant and tolerant man who understood how universal human motives can betray ordinary people into behaving badly. In this sonnet, he throws up his hands at the destruction brought about by sexual desire.

Polly Perkins

ANONYMOUS

I am a broken-hearted milkman, in grief I'm arrayed,
Through keeping of the company of a young servant maid,
Who lived on board and wages the house to keep clean
In a gentleman's family near Paddington Green.

Chorus:
    She was as beautiful as a butterfly
        And as proud as a Queen
    Was pretty little Polly Perkins of
        Paddington Green.

She'd an ankle like an antelope and a step like a deer,
A voice like a blackbird, so mellow and clear,
Her hair hung in ringlets, so beautiful and long,
I thought that she loved me but I found I was wrong.

When I'd rattle in the morning and cry 'milk below',
At the sound of my milk-cans her face she would show
With a smile upon her countenance and a laugh in her eye,
If I thought she'd have loved me, I'd have laid down to die.

When I asked her to marry me she said 'Oh! what stuff'.
And told me to 'drop it, for she'd had quite enough
Of my nonsense' – at the same time I'd been very kind,
But to marry a milkman she didn't feel inclined.

'Oh, the man that has me must have silver and gold,
A chariot to ride in and be handsome and bold,
His hair must be curly as any watch spring,
And his whiskers as big as a brush for clothing.'

The words that she uttered went straight through my heart,
I sobbed, I sighed, and straight did depart;
With a tear in my eyelid as big as a bean,
Bidding good-bye to Polly and Paddington Green.

In six months she married, – this hard-hearted girl, –
But it was not a Wi-count, and it was not a Nearl,
It was not a 'Baronite', but a shade or two wuss,
It was a bow-legged conductor of a twopenny bus.

*The Victorian Age is rich in songs and ballads intended for the music-hall or
smoking-concert. The writers were not among the gentry and chose their
subjects accordingly. This example, whose tune survives, is the work of someone
with enough skill and feelings for words to make it worth while as a comic
poem in its own right.*

121

The Old Stoic

EMILY BRONTË

Riches I hold in light esteem,
And Love I laugh to scorn;
And lust of Fame was but a dream
That vanished with the morn –

And if I pray, the only prayer
That moves my lips for me
Is – 'Leave the heart that now I bear,
And give me liberty.'

Yes, as my swift days near their goal,
'Tis all that I implore –
In life and death, a chainless soul,
With courage to endure!

A stoic in ancient times was one of a school of philosophers advocating self-control and indifference to pleasure and pain. The word has always implied brave endurance of suffering. Emily Brontë, cooped up in Haworth Parsonage, near Bradford, with her sisters and dying of consumption at the age of 30, deserved the name.

Concord Hymn

RALPH WALDO EMERSON

By the rude bridge that arched the flood,
Their flag to April's breeze unfurled,
Here once the embattled farmers stood,
And fired the shot heard round the world.

The foe long since in silence slept;
Alike the conqueror silent sleeps;
And Time the ruined bridge has swept
Down the dark stream which seaward creeps.

On this green bank by this soft stream,
We set to-day a votive stone;
That memory may their deed redeem,
When, like our sires, our sons are gone.

Spirit, that made those heroes dare
To die, or leave their children free,
Bid Time and Nature gently spare
The shaft we raise to them and thee.

Concord was the village in Massachusetts where in 1775 the first engagement of the American War of Independence took place. In 1837 a granite obelisk was erected there and Emerson wrote this poem for the occasion. It is offered this month in salute to the United States of America and its people on their national day.

To Celia

BEN JONSON

Drink to me only with thine eyes,
　　And I will pledge with mine;
Or leave a kiss but in the cup,
　　And I'll not look for wine.
The thirst that from the soul doth rise
　　Doth ask a drink divine;
But might I of Jove's nectar sup,
　　I would not change for thine.
I sent thee late a rosy wreath,
　　Not so much honouring thee
As giving it a hope that there
　　It could not withered be;
But thou thereon didst only breathe,
　　And sent'st it back to me;
Since when it grows, and smells, I swear,
　　Not of itself, but thee!

*This is, or was, one of the most famous of all English songs. The splendid tune
that goes with it is old but not as old as the words, probably about the middle of
the eighteenth century. In the seventh and eighth lines the poet says the exact
opposite of what he means, but his obvious earnestness carries him through.*

On Wenlock Edge

A. E. HOUSMAN

On Wenlock Edge the wood's in trouble;
    His forest fleece the Wrekin heaves;
The gale, it plies the saplings double,
    And thick on Severn snow the leaves.

'Twould blow like this through holt and hanger
    When Uricon the city stood:
'Tis the old wind in the old anger,
    But then it threshed another wood.

Then, 'twas before my time, the Roman
    At yonder heaving hill would stare:
The blood that warms an English yeoman,
    The thoughts that hurt him, they were there.

There, like the wind through woods in riot,
    Through him the gale of life blew high;
The tree of man was never quiet:
    Then 'twas the Roman, now 'tis I.

The gale, it plies the saplings double,
    It blows so hard, 'twill soon be gone:
To-day the Roman and his trouble
    Are ashes under Uricon.

Housman's first book of poems was called A Shropshire Lad. That 'lad' is a fictitious character, but although Housman himself had no particular roots in that county, he worked hard and successfully in his poems to make the background real. So here Wenlock Edge and the Wrekin are real hilly places and Uricon or Viroconium is a real vanished Roman town.

125 High Summer on the Mountains

IDRIS DAVIES

High summer on the mountains
And on the clover leas,
And on the local sidings,
And on the rhubarb leaves.

Brass bands in all the valleys
Blaring defiant tunes,
Crowds, acclaiming carnival,
Prize pigs and wooden spoons.

Dust on shabby hedgerows
Behind the colliery wall,
Dust on rail and girder
And tram and prop and all.

High summer on the slag heaps
And on polluted streams,
And old men in the morning
Telling the town their dreams.

At the beginning of this concentrated and deceptively simple-seeming poem the little-known Idris Davies seems to be promising a conventional hymn to summer, but by the end of the first verse we realise that these are very much not the mountains of romance. This kind of tram, of course, carries coal not people.

Evening Prayer

THOMAS KEN

Glory to Thee, my God, this night
For all the blessings of the light;
Keep me, O keep me, King of kings,
Beneath Thine own almighty wings.

Forgive me, Lord, for Thy dear Son,
The ill that I this day have done,
That with the world, myself, and Thee
I, ere I sleep, at peace may be.

Teach me to live, that I may dread
The grave as little as my bed;
Teach me to die, that so I may
Rise glorious at the awful day.

O may my soul on Thee repose,
And with sweet sleep mine eyelids close,
Sleep that may me more vigorous make
To serve my God when I awake.

When in the night I sleepless lie,
My soul with heavenly thoughts supply;
Let no ill dreams disturb my rest,
No powers of darkness me molest.

Praise God, from Whom all blessings flow,
Praise Him, all creatures here below,
Praise Him above, ye heav'nly host,
Praise Father, Son and Holy Ghost.

The churchman who wrote this poem had a difficult and even dangerous career,
being closely involved in the political troubles surrounding the expulsion of
King James II and the accession of William of Orange in 1688–9.
Nobody could guess anything like that from the impressively simple
words of this once-famous hymn.

'De Gustibus —'

127

ROBERT BROWNING

Your ghost will walk, you lover of trees,
  (If our loves remain)
  In an English lane,
By a cornfield-side a-flutter with poppies.
Hark, those two in the hazel coppice –
A boy and a girl, if the good fates please,
  Making love, say, –
  The happier they!
Draw yourself up from the light of the moon,
And let them pass, as they will too soon,
  With the bean-flowers' boon,
  And the blackbird's tune,
  And May, and June!

What I love best in all the world
Is a castle, precipice-encurled,
In a gash of the wind-grieved Apennine.
Or look for me, old fellow of mine,
(If I get my head from out of the mouth
O' the grave, and loose my spirit's bands,
And come again to the land of lands) –
In a sea-side house to the farther South,
Where the baked cicala dies of drouth,
And one sharp tree – 'tis a cypress – stands,
By the many hundred years red-rusted,
Rough iron-spiked, ripe fruit-o'ercrusted,
My sentinel to guard the sands
To the water's edge. For, what expands
Before the house, but the great opaque
Blue breadth of sea without a break?

    . . . . . .

  Italy, my Italy!
Queen Mary's saying serves for me –
  (When fortune's malice
  Lost her – Calais) –

Open my heart and you will see
Graved inside of it, 'Italy.'
Such lovers old are I and she:
So it always was, so shall ever be!

*The title is part of a Latin proverb meaning, roughly, there can be no argument
about tastes. So Browning's friend likes England best while he himself prefers
Italy – this is one of his sharpest pictures of life in the sun. Sadly, it was never
the same to him after his wife died there, and he was settled back in London
before he was 40.*

Shall I Compare Thee to a Summer's Day?

128

WILLIAM SHAKESPEARE

Shall I compare thee to a summer's day?
Thou art more lovely and more temperate:
Rough winds do shake the darling buds of May,
And summer's lease hath all too short a date:
Sometime too hot the eye of heaven shines,
And often is his gold complexion dimm'd:
And every fair from fair sometime declines,
By chance, or nature's changing course, untrimm'd:
But thy eternal summer shall not fade,
Nor lose possession of that fair thou owest;
Nor shall Death brag thou wander'st in his shade,
When in eternal lines to time thou growest:
    So long as men can breathe, or eyes can see,
    So long lives this, and this gives life to thee.

*Shakespeare's opening lines are often irresistible and instantly taken in, but the
going can get a little more difficult further on. Here, the first 'fair' means
something like 'fair creature', the second and third 'excellence, beauty'. In
Elizabethan English the verb 'to owe' was sometimes used in the related
meaning of 'to own'.*

The Owl

129

EDWARD THOMAS

Downhill I came, hungry, and yet not starved;
Cold, yet had heat within me that was proof
Against the North wind; tired, yet so that rest
Had seemed the sweetest thing under a roof.

Then at the inn I had food, fire, and rest,
Knowing how hungry, cold, and tired was I.
All of the night was quite barred out except
An owl's cry, a most melancholy cry.

Shaken out long and clear upon the hill,
No merry note, nor cause of merriment,
But one telling me plain what I escaped
And others could not, that night, as in I went.

And salted was my food, and my repose,
Salted and sobered, too, by the bird's voice
Speaking for all who lay under the stars,
Soldiers and poor, unable to rejoice.

Although Thomas saw service enough before being killed on the Western Front,
he never tackles the war head-on as a subject. The most he does is let a hint of it
through, as here. He has the gift of writing in such a direct way that when he
says he feels something, the reader is in no doubt that he actually does feel it.

The Tiger

WILLIAM BLAKE

Tiger! Tiger! burning bright
In the forests of the night,
What immortal hand or eye
Could frame thy fearful symmetry?

In what distant deeps or skies
Burnt the fire of thine eyes?
On what wings dare he aspire?
What the hand dare seize the fire?

And what shoulder, and what art,
Could twist the sinews of thy heart?
And when thy heart began to beat,
What dread hand? And what dread feet?

What the hammer? What the chain?
In what furnace was thy brain?
What the anvil? What dread grasp
Dare its deadly terrors clasp?

When the stars threw down their spears,
And watered heaven with their tears,
Did he smile his work to see?
Did he who made the Lamb make thee?

Tiger! Tiger! burning bright
In the forests of the night,
What immortal hand or eye
Dare frame thy fearful symmetry?

When I read this marvellous poem as a boy I thought Blake meant that the tiger was literally burning, giving off flames, was a supernatural being. I had it wrong; it is one of God's creatures – that in fact is the whole point. But I still cannot really understand about the burning, nor later about the dread feet.

131 Our God, Our Help in Ages Past

ISAAC WATTS

Our God, our help in ages past,
  Our hope for years to come,
Our shelter from the stormy blast,
  And our eternal home.

Under the shadow of thy throne
  Thy saints have dwelt secure;
Sufficient is thine arm alone,
  And our defence is sure.

Before the hills in order stood,
  Or earth receiv'd her frame;
From everlasting thou art God
  To endless years the same.

   .   .   .   .   .   .

A thousand ages in thy sight,
  Are like an evening gone;
Short as the watch that ends the night
  Before the rising sun.

The busy tribes of flesh and blood,
  With all their lives and cares,
Are carried downwards by thy flood,
  And lost in following years.

Time like an ever-rolling stream
  Bears all its sons away;
They fly forgotten as a dream
  Dies at the opening day.

Like flowery fields the nations stand
  Pleas'd with the morning light;
The flowers beneath the mower's hand
  Lie withering ere 'tis night.

Our God, our help in ages past,
Our hope for years to come,
Be thou our guard while troubles last,
And our eternal home.

This most famous of all hymns is printed here in a fuller version than the one usually sung. Watts, a Nonconformist pastor, wrote many others and also published sermons, theological works and moral poems for children. He was a charitable man who for many years gave a third of his limited income to the poor.

Break, Break, Break 132

ALFRED, LORD TENNYSON

Break, break, break,
On thy cold gray stones, O Sea!
And I would that my tongue could utter
The thoughts that arise in me.

O well for the fisherman's boy,
That he shouts with his sister at play!
O well for the sailor lad,
That he sings in his boat on the bay!

And the stately ships go on
To their haven under the hill;
But O for the touch of a vanished hand,
And the sound of a voice that is still!

Break, break, break,
At the foot of thy crags, O Sea!
But the tender grace of a day that is dead
Will never come back to me.

Some time ago this was one of those poems that a great many people seemed to know, or to know a few phrases of, perhaps without ever knowing who wrote it. But of course it is very characteristic of 'the saddest of all English poets', with its quiet opening that leads to a burst of passion just after the halfway mark.

Seaside Golf

SIR JOHN BETJEMAN

How straight it flew, how long it flew,
　　It clear'd the rutty track
And soaring, disappeared from view
　　Beyond the bunker's back –
A glorious, sailing, bounding drive
That made me glad I was alive.

And down the fairway, far along
　　It glowed a lonely white;
I played an iron sure and strong
　　And clipp'd it out of sight,
And spite of grassy banks between
I knew I'd find it on the green.

And so I did. It lay content
　　Two paces from the pin;
A steady putt and then it went
　　Oh, most securely in.
That very turf rejoiced to see
That quite unprecedented three.

Ah! seaweed smells from sandy caves
　　And thyme and mist in whiffs,
In-coming tide, Atlantic waves
　　Slapping the sunny cliffs,
Lark song and sea sounds in the air
And splendour, splendour everywhere.

Not many of Sir John's poems illustrate better than this one his great power of
moving from the ordinary to the sublime in a short space. One moment a
common-place little man is knocking his golf ball along and the next there is
'splendour everywhere' – real splendour, too, beautifully imagined and put
together.

This Time of Year a Twelvemonth Past

A. E. HOUSMAN

This time of year a twelvemonth past,
  When Fred and I would meet,
We needs must jangle, till at last
  We fought and I was beat.

So then the summer fields about,
  Till rainy days began,
Rose Harland on her Sundays out
  Walked with the better man.

The better man she walks with still,
  Though now 'tis not with Fred:
A lad that lives and has his will
  Is worth a dozen dead.

Fred keeps the house all kinds of weather;
  And clay's the house he keeps;
When Rose and I walk out together
  Stock-still lies Fred and sleeps.

This poem comes from Housman's first volume, A Shropshire Lad, which
first appeared in 1896. (He only published one other in his lifetime.) As often
he invents a simple story and makes a grim reflection on it. Another writer
might have taken against Rose for her change of heart; Housman simply
accepts it.

The Foggy, Foggy Dew

135

ANONYMOUS

When I was a bachelor, I lived by myself
And I worked at the weaver's trade;
The only, only thing that I ever did wrong
Was to woo a fair young maid.
I wooed her in the winter time,
And in the summer too;
And the only, only thing I ever did wrong
Was to keep her from the foggy, foggy dew.

One night she came to my bedside
Where I lay fast asleep;
She laid her head upon my bed,
And then began to weep.
She sighed, she cried, she damn near died,
She said – 'What shall I do?' –
So I hauled her into bed and I covered up her head,
Just to save her from the foggy, foggy dew.

Oh, I am a bachelor, I live with my son,
And we work at the weaver's trade;
And every, every time that I look into his eyes,
He reminds me of that maid.
He reminds me of the winter time.
And of the summer too;
And the many, many times that I held her in my arms,
Just to keep her from the foggy, foggy dew.

This song, well known at one time, perhaps even to this day, probably dates
from the late nineteenth century, but it seems not to have been written down till
the 'Thirties. What has caused it to survive must be the pretty tune that goes so
well with the words and the engaging mixture of innocence and naughtiness in
those words.

Death the Leveller

JAMES SHIRLEY

The glories of our blood and state
    Are shadows, not substantial things;
There is no armour against Fate;
    Deaths lays his icy hand on Kings:
        Sceptre and Crown
        Must tumble down,
And in the dust be equal made
With the poor crooked scythe and spade.

Some men with swords may reap the field,
    And plant fresh laurels where they kill:
But their strong nerves at last must yield;
    They tame but one another still:
        Early or late
        They stoop to fate,
And must give up their murmuring breath
When they, pale captives, creep to death.

The garlands wither on your brow;
    Then boast no more your mighty deeds!
Upon Death's purple altar now
    See where the victor-victim bleeds.
        Your heads must come
        To the cold tomb:
Only the actions of the just
Smell sweet and blossom in their dust.

Shirley was a schoolmaster and a playwright. This song, or dirge, is the epilogue to one of his dramatic pieces and is supposed to have terrified Oliver Cromwell, though the King would have it sung to him. Shirley and his wife died of shock and exposure on the occasion of the Great Fire of London.

137 # A Dream Within a Dream

EDGAR ALLAN POE

Take this kiss upon the brow!
And, in parting from you now,
Thus much let me avow –
You are not wrong, who deem
That my days have been a dream;
Yet if hope has flown away
In a night, or in a day,
In a vision, or in none,
Is it therefore the less gone?
All that we see or seem
Is but a dream within a dream.

I stand amid the roar
Of a surf-tormented shore,
And I hold within my hand
Grains of the golden sand –
How few! yet how they creep
Through my fingers to the deep,
While I weep – while I weep!
Oh God! can I not grasp
Them with a tighter clasp?
Oh God! can I not save
One from the pitiless wave?
Is all that we see or seem
But a dream within a dream?

For most people Poe's name conjures up visions of horrific murders and sinister
hauntings, but he also wrote poems of a kind of extreme romanticism for which
dreamy seems just the word. In fact, the title of this one sums up his view of life,
at least while he was writing poetry. At other times he gambled or got drunk.

The Song of the Western Men 138

ROBERT STEPHEN HAWKER

A good sword and a trusty hand!
    A merry heart and true!
King James's men shall understand
    What Cornish lads can do.

And have they fix'd the where and when?
    And shall Trelawny die?
Here's twenty thousand Cornish men
    Will see the reason why!

Out spake their captain brave and bold,
    A merry wight was he:
'If London Tower were Michael's hold,
    We'll set Trelawny free!

'We'll cross the Tamar, land to land,
    The Severn is no stay,
All side by side, and hand to hand,
    And who shall bid us nay?

'And when we come to London Wall,
    A pleasant sight to view,
Come forth! come forth! ye cowards all,
    To better men than you!

'Trelawny he's in keep and hold,
    Trelawny he may die;
But twenty thousand Cornish bold
    Will see the reason why!'

Robert Stephen Hawker was vicar of a Cornish village and an antiquarian as
well as a poet. He writes here of an episode in 1688 when Bishop Trelawney, a
Cornishman, was held in the Tower for plotting against the King (soon
released) – a forgotten story brought to life by Hawker's energy and force. Ever
since 1688, and until quite recently, lines 6–8 were a popular saying in
Cornwall.

139 *When We Two Parted*

GEORGE GORDON, LORD BYRON

When we two parted
  In silence and tears,
Half broken-hearted
  To sever for years,
Pale grew thy cheek and cold,
  Colder thy kiss;
Truly that hour foretold
  Sorrow to this.

The dew of the morning
  Sunk chill on my brow –
It felt like the warning
  Of what I feel now.
Thy vows are all broken,
  And light is thy fame;
I hear thy name spoken,
  And share in its shame.

They name thee before me,
  A knell to mine ear;
A shudder comes o'er me –
  Why wert thou so dear?
They know not I knew thee,
  Who knew thee too well: –
Long, long shall I rue thee,
  Too deeply to tell.

In secret we met –
  In silence I grieve
That thy heart could forget,
  Thy spirit deceive.
If I should meet thee
  After long years,
How should I greet thee? –
  With silence and tears.

Byron's amatory career was what is sometimes called a stormy one, with plenty of scenes and separations. This poem may of course be the product of a real event, but nothing is known. For all its power and authority, the portrayal of dignified grief is perhaps a little marred by the air of moral sniffiness at a couple of points.

I Am

JOHN CLARE

I am: yet what I am none cares or knows.
　　My friends forsake me like a memory lost;
I am the self-consumer of my woes,
　　They rise and vanish in oblivious host,
Like shades in love and death's oblivion lost;
And yet I am, and live with shadows tost

Into the nothingness of scorn and noise,
　　Into the living sea of waking dreams,
Where there is neither sense of life nor joys,
　　But the vast shipwreck of my life's esteems;
And e'en the dearest – that I loved the best –
Are strange – nay, rather stranger than the rest.

I long for scenes where man has never trod,
　　A place where woman never smiled or wept;
There to abide with my Creator, God,
　　And sleep as I in childhood sweetly slept:
Untroubling and untroubled where I lie,
　　The grass below – above the vaulted sky.

Clare, once known as the Northamptonshire Peasant Poet, was a gardener and farm labourer and wrote about the countryside and village life. He became insane in his mid-forties and was put away. He is supposed to have written this poem in Northampton County Asylum, where he was confined until his death.

141
The World Is Too Much with Us

WILLIAM WORDSWORTH

The world is too much with us; late and soon,
Getting and spending, we lay waste our powers:
Little we see in Nature that is ours;
We have given out hearts away, a sordid boon!
The Sea that bares her bosom to the moon;
The winds that will be howling at all hours,
And are up-gathered now like sleeping flowers;
For this, for everything, we are out of tune;
It moves us not. – Great God! I'd rather be
A Pagan suckled in a creed outworn;
So might I, standing on this pleasant lea,
Have glimpses that would make me less forlorn;
Have sight of Proteus rising from the sea;
Or hear old Triton blow his wreathèd horn.

Wordsworth is usually thought of as our best writer of sonnets after Shakespeare and Milton. This one is very much a public poem, an address to the nation; he was appointed Poet Laureate in 1843. He argues here that a pagan, however benighted, has the benefit of believing in romantic figures like the two sea-gods.

from
In Memoriam

ALFRED, LORD TENNYSON

Unwatched, the garden bough shall sway,
　　The tender blossom flutter down,
　　Unloved, that beech will gather brown,
This maple burn itself away;

Unloved, the sun-flower, shining fair,
　　Ray round with flames her disk of seed,
　　And many a rose-carnation feed
With summer spice the humming air;

Unloved, by many a sandy bar,
　　The brook shall babble down the plain,
　　At noon or when the lesser wain
Is twisting round the polar star;

Uncared for, gird the windy grove,
　　And flood the haunts of hern and crake;
　　Or into silver arrows break
The sailing moon in creek and cove;

Till from the garden and the wild
　　A fresh association blow,
　　And year by year the landscape grow
Familiar to the stranger's child;

As year by year the labourer tills
　　His wonted glebe, or lops the glades;
　　And year by year our memory fades
From all the circle of the hills.

This extract refers to the departure of the Tennyson family from the house in
Somersby, Lincolnshire, where Alfred had been born 28 years earlier. It
captures the familiar feeling that whoever comes here next will not value the
place so well, and beyond that the more sombre reflection that in time none of
us will be remembered anywhere.

143 # 'For All We Have and Are': 1914

RUDYARD KIPLING

For all we have and are,
For all our children's fate,
Stand up and take the war.
The Hun is at the gate!
Our world has passed away,
In wantoness o'erthrown.
There is nothing left to-day
But steel and fire and stone!
    Though all we knew depart,
    The old Commandments stand: –
    'In courage keep your heart,
    In strength lift up your hand.'

Once more we hear the word
That sickened earth of old: –
'No law except the Sword
Unsheathed and uncontrolled.'
Once more it knits mankind,
Once more the nations go
To meet and break and bind
A crazed and driven foe.

Comfort, content, delight,
The ages' slow-bought gain,
They shrivelled in a night.
Only ourselves remain
To face the naked days
In silent fortitude,
Through perils and dismays
Renewed and re-renewed.
    Though all we made depart,
    The old Commandments stand: –
    'In patience keep your heart,
    In strength lift up your hand.'

No easy hope or lies
Shall bring us to our goal,
But iron sacrifice
Of body, will and soul.
There is but one task for all –
One life for each to give.
What stands if Freedom fall?
Who dies if England live?

Kipling wrote this poem within the first month of Britain's entry into the Great War. Unlike some of his contemporaries he foresaw a long bitter struggle. 'The Hun' is not a racialist reference but a way of saying that civilisation is under threat from barbarism.

It Rains 144

EDWARD THOMAS

It rains, and nothing stirs within the fence
Anywhere through the orchard's untrodden, dense
Forest of parsley. The great diamonds
Of rain on the grassblades there is none to break,
Or the fallen petals further down to shake.

And I am nearly as happy as possible
To search the wilderness in vain though well,
To think of two walking, kissing there,
Drenched, yet forgetting the kisses of the rain:
Sad, too, to think that never, never again,

Unless alone, so happy shall I walk
In the rain. When I turn away, on its fine stalk
Twilight has fined to naught, the parsley flower
Figures, suspended still and ghostly white,
The past hovering as it revisits the light.

Thomas's friend and fellow-poet Walter de la Mare said of him that he had unlearned all literary influences, and it is certainly true that there is nothing in his poetry that recalls any earlier writer. De la Mare also said that he had 'never heard English used so fastidiously and yet so unaffectedly' as in Thomas's talk – a judgement that applies to his poems too.

Romance

WALTER JAMES TURNER

When I was but thirteen or so
I went into a golden land;
Chimborazo, Cotopaxi
Took me by the hand.

My father died, my brother too,
They passed like fleeting dreams.
I stood where Popocatapetl
In the sunlight gleams.

I dimly heard the master's voice
And boys far-off at play;
Chimborazo, Cotopaxi
Had stolen me away.

I walked in a great golden dream
To and fro from school –
Shining Popocatapetl
The dusty streets did rule.

I walked home with a gold dark boy
And never a word I'd say;
Chimborazo, Cotopaxi
Had taken my speech away:

I gazed entranced upon his face
Fairer than any flower –
O shining Popocatapetl,
It was thy magic hour:

The houses, people, traffic seemed
Thin fading dreams by day;
Chimborazo, Cotopaxi,
They had stolen my soul away!

Born in Australia, Walter James Turner wrote a great deal in various literary
forms, but he is mostly known today for this one poem. Chimborazo and
Cotopaxi are peaks in the Andes and Popocatépetl (smoking mountain) is a
volcano in Mexico, but of course the sound and the exotic mysteriousness are
what count.

To Night

PERCY BYSSHE SHELLEY

Swiftly walk o'er the western wave,
    Spirit of Night!
Out of the misty eastern cave,
Where, all the long and lone daylight,
Thou wovest dreams of joy and fear,
Which make thee terrible and dear, –
    Swift be thy flight!

Wrap thy form in a mantle gray,
    Star-inwrought!
Blind with thine hair the eyes of Day;
Kiss her until she be wearied out,
Then wander o'er city, and sea, and land,
Touching all with thine opiate wand –
    Come, long-sought!

When I arose and saw the dawn,
    I sighed for thee;
When light rode high, and the dew was gone,
And noon lay heavy on flower and tree,
And the weary Day turned to his rest,
Lingering like an unloved guest,
    I sighed for thee.

Thy brother Death came, and cried,
    Wouldst thou me?
Thy sweet child Sleep, the filmy-eyed,
Murmured like a noon-tide bee,
Shall I nestle near thy side?
Wouldst thou me? – And I replied,
    No, not thee!

Death will come when thou art dead,
    Soon, too soon –
Sleep will come when thou art fled;
Of neither would I ask the boon
I ask of thee, belovèd Night –
Swift be thine approaching flight,
    Come soon, soon!

*In the course of his short life Shelley tried his hand at most kinds of poetry.
Much of it is intellectual, concerned with abstract ideas, but he wrote a few
lyrics that, like this one, make a strong impression by their atmosphere rather
than their meaning.*

Slough

SIR JOHN BETJEMAN

Come, friendly bombs, and fall on Slough,
It isn't fit for humans now,
There isn't grass to graze a cow
    Swarm over, Death!

Come, bombs, and blow to smithereens
Those air-conditioned, bright canteens,
Tinned fruit, tinned meat, tinned milk, tinned beans
    Tinned minds, tinned breath.

Mess up the mess they call a town –
A house for ninety-seven down
And once a week a half-a-crown
    For twenty years,

And get that man with double chin
Who'll always cheat and always win,
Who washes his repulsive skin
    In women's tears,

And smash his desk of polished oak
And smash his hands so used to stroke
And stop his boring dirty joke
    And make him yell.

But spare the bald young clerks who add
The profits of the stinking cad;
It's not their fault that they are mad,
    They've tasted Hell.

It's not their fault they do not know
The birdsong from the radio,
It's not their fault they often go
    To Maidenhead

And talk of sports and makes of cars
In various bogus Tudor bars
And daren't look up and see the stars
    But belch instead.

In labour-saving homes, with care
Their wives frizz out peroxide hair
And dry it in synthetic air
    And paint their nails.

Come, friendly bombs, and fall on Slough
To get it ready for the plough.
The cabbages are coming now;
    The earth exhales.

In his poetry John Betjeman was not always the amiable and tolerant observer
of urban and suburban life he often seems. He had a sharp eye for packaged
food and packaged culture and for squalid behaviour and could, as here, give
them a battering – though never without humour. The poem dates from the
mid-'Thirties, well before any real bombs came.

Bermudas

148

ANDREW MARVELL

Where the remote Bermudas ride
In the ocean's bosom unespied,
From a small boat, that rowed along,
The listening winds received this song.
    'What should we do but sing his praise
That led us through the watery maze,
Unto an isle so long unknown,
And yet far kinder than our own?
Where he the huge sea-monsters wracks,
That lift the deep upon their backs.
He lands us on a grassy stage,
Safe from the storms' and prelates' rage.
He gave us this eternal spring,
Which here enamels everything;
And sends the fowls to us in care,
On daily visits through the air.
He hangs in shades the orange bright,
Like golden lamps in a green night,
And does in the pomegranates close
Jewels more rich than Ormus shows.
He makes the figs our mouths to meet,
And throws the melons at our feet;
But apples plants of such a price
No tree could ever bear them twice.
With cedars, chosen by his hand,
From Lebanon, he stores the land;

[continued]

And makes the hollow seas that roar
Proclaim the ambergris on shore.
He cast (of which we rather boast)
The Gospel's pearl upon our coast,
And in these rocks for us did frame
A temple, where to sound his Name.
Oh let our voice in his praise exalt,
Till it arrive at heaven's vault,
Which thence, perhaps, rebounding may
Echo beyond the Mexique Bay.'
    Thus sung they, in the English boat,
An holy and a cheerful note,
And all the way, to guide their chime,
With falling oars they kept the time.

*Marvell was a considerable politician, becoming MP for Hull from 1659. The
Pilgrim Fathers had landed in Plymouth Bay, Massachusetts, only the year
before he was born, and the Bermudas themselves in the North Atlantic had
had their first British settlers not much earlier. The New World was still very
new and, as this poem shows, believed to be full of wonders.*

149

Tom Bowling

CHARLES DIBDIN

Here, a sheer hulk, lies poor Tom Bowling,
The darling of our crew;
No more he'll hear the tempest howling,
For death has broach'd him to.
His form was of the manliest beauty,
His heart was kind and soft,
Faithful below he did his duty,
And now he's gone aloft.

Tom never from his word departed,
His virtues were so rare,
His friends were many, and true hearted,
His Poll was kind and fair:
And then he'd sing so blithe and jolly,
Ah many's the time and oft!
But mirth is turn'd to melancholy,
For Tom is gone aloft.

Yet shall Poor Tom find pleasant weather,
When he who all commands
Shall give, to call life's crew together,
The word to pipe all hands.
Thus death, who Kings and Tars dispatches,
In vain Tom's life has doffed,
For, though his body's under hatches,
His soul is gone aloft.

*Dibdin was a musician, actor and variety entertainer. He wrote this famous
song in tribute to his brother, Capt. Thomas Dibdin. Charles seems to have
thought a sheer hulk was a dismasted wreck or lifeless lump; in fact it was a
floating crane-platform – but call that poetic licence.*

Lyarde   150

JOHN LYDGATE

Lyarde is an old horse and can naught well draw;
He shall be put into the park holly for to gnaw.
Barefoot withouten shoon there shall he go,
For he is an old horse and can no more do.
Whiles that Lyarde could draw, the whiles was he loved;
They put him to provender, and therewith he throve.
Now he can naught do his deed as he could beforn,
They lay before him pea-straw, and bear away the corn.
They led him to the smithy to pull off his shoon
And put him to greenwood, there for to gone.
Whoso can naught do his deed, he shall to park.
Barefoot withouten shoon, and go with Lyarde.

*In the Middle Ages writers went in for bulk or length; Lydgate is said to have
written more than a million lines of verse. Not surprisingly, perhaps, even his
best-known works lack something. But this lament for old age is still fresh. I
have modernised it only as much as was needed to make it intelligible.*

151

Sweet and Low

ALFRED, LORD TENNYSON

Sweet and low, sweet and low,
　　Wind of the western sea,
Low, low, breathe and blow,
　　Wind of the western sea!
Over the rolling waters go,
Come from the dying moon, and blow,
　　Blow him again to me;
While my little one, while my pretty one, sleeps.

Sleep and rest, sleep and rest,
　　Father will come to thee soon;
Rest, rest, on mother's breast,
　　Father will come to thee soon;
Father will come to his babe in the nest,
Silver sails all out of the west
　　Under the silver moon;
Sleep, my little one, sleep, my pretty one, sleep.

Alternative Version

　　Bright is the moon on the deep,
Bright are the cliffs in her beam,
　　Sleep, my little one, sleep!
Look he smiles, and opens his hands,
He sees his father in distant lands,
And kisses him there in a dream,
　　Sleep, sleep.

　　Father is over the deep,
Father will come to thee soon,
　　Sleep, my pretty one, sleep!
Father will come to his babe in the nest,
Silver sails all out of the West,
Under the silver moon,
　　Sleep, sleep!

This famous lullaby, from The Princess, *suggests music with its very words. Tennyson wrote two versions of it and sent them to his mother to choose which should be published. She picked the one she considered 'more songlike', and he followed her choice. Nobody is likely to quarrel, though the alternative version is a fair enough poem.*

The Listeners

WALTER DE LA MARE

'Is there anybody there?' said the Traveller,
   Knocking on the moonlit door;
And his horse in the silence champed the grasses
   Of the forest's ferny floor:
And a bird flew up out of the turret,
   Above the Traveller's head:
And he smote upon the door again a second time;
   'Is there anybody there?' he said.
But no one descended to the Traveller;
   No head from the leaf-fringed sill
Leaned over and looked into his grey eyes,
   Where he stood perplexed and still.
But only a host of phantom listeners
   That dwelt in the lone house then
Stood listening in the quiet of the moonlight
   To that voice from the world of men:
Stood thronging the faint moonbeams on the dark stair,
   That goes down to the empty hall,
Hearkening in an air stirred and shaken
   By the lonely Traveller's call.
And he felt in his heart their strangeness,
   Their stillness answering his cry,
While his horse moved, cropping the dark turf,
   'Neath the starred and leafy sky;
For he suddenly smote on the door, even
   Louder, and lifted his head: –
'Tell them I came, and no one answered,
   That I kept my word,' he said.
Never the least stir made the listeners,
   Though every word he spake
Fell echoing through the shadowiness of the still house
   From the one man left awake:
Ay, they heard his foot upon the stirrup,
   And the sound of iron on stone,
And how the silence surged softly backward,
   When the plunging hoofs were gone.

De la Mare wrote very effective stories of the macabre but he is valued more for
his highly individual poems – short for the most part, simple in language,
fanciful, often dream-like or seeming to recall some lost folk-tale. This is his
best known, fully understandable in one way, and yet leaving a mystery
unexplained.

Summer

CHRISTINA ROSSETTI

Winter is cold-hearted,
    Spring is yea and nay,
Autumn is a weathercock
    Blown every way.
Summer days for me
When every leaf is on its tree;

When Robin's not a beggar,
    And Jenny Wren's a bride,
And larks hang singing, singing, singing,
    Over the wheat-fields wide,
    And anchored lilies ride,
And the pendulum spider
    Swings from side to side;

And blue-black beetles transact business,
    And gnats fly in a host,
And furry caterpillars hasten
    That no time be lost,
And moths grow fat and thrive,
And ladybirds arrive.

Before green apples blush,
    Before green nuts embrown,
Why, one day in the country
    Is worth a month in town;
    Is worth a day and a year
Of the dusty, musty, lag-last fashion
    That days drone elsewhere.

*Nobody appreciates the country more than those who spend very nearly all their
time in London, like Christina who was born in Charlotte Street and lived for
years in Euston Square. And nobody has a greater feeling for summer than
those shivering in the depths of winter – this sunny poem is dated
15 January 1864.*

The Parish Work-House 154

GEORGE CRABBE

Their's is yon House that holds the Parish Poor,
Whose walls of mud scarce bear the broken door;
There, where the putrid vapours flagging, play,
And the dull wheel hums doleful through the day; –
There Children dwell who know no Parents' care;
Parents, who know no Children's love, dwell there;
Heart-broken Matrons on their joyless bed,
Forsaken Wives and Mothers never wed;
Dejected Widows with unheeded tears,
And crippled Age with more than childhood fears;
The Lame the Blind, and, far the happiest they!
The moping Idiot and the Madman gay.
Here too the Sick their final doom receive,
Here brought amid the scenes of grief, to grieve;
Where the loud groans from some sad chamber flow,
Mixt with the clamours of the crowd below;
Here sorrowing, they each kindred sorrow scan,
And the cold charities of man to man:
Whose laws indeed for ruin'd Age provide,
And strong compulsion plucks the scrap from pride;
But still that scrap is bought with many a sigh,
And pride embitters what it can't deny.
　　Say ye, opprest by some fantastic woes,
Some jarring nerve that baffles your repose;
Who press the downy couch, while slaves advance
With timid eye, to read the distant glance;
Who with sad prayers the weary Doctor tease,
To name the nameless ever-new disease;
Who with mock patience dire complaints endure,
Which real pain and that alone can cure;
How would ye bear in real pain to lie,
Despis'd, neglected, left alone to die?
How would ye bear to draw your latest breath,
Where all that's wretched paves the way for death?

Crabbe was a Suffolk day-labourer who became a parson and a successful poet.
He knew rural life intimately, not least its unattractive and painful aspects, as
is shown in this extract from his long poem The Village. His passion for truth
and his unerring eye for detail made him one of the first and greatest of
English realists.

Three War Poems

SIEGFRIED SASSOON

Attack

At dawn the ridge emerges massed and dun
In the wild purple of the glow'ring sun,
Smouldering through spouts of drifting smoke that shroud
The menacing scarred slope; and, one by one,
Tanks creep and topple forward to the wire.
The barrage roars and lifts. Then, clumsily bowed
With bombs and guns and shovels and battle-gear,
Men jostle and climb to meet the bristling fire.
Lines of grey, muttering faces, masked with fear,
They leave their trenches, going over the top,
While time ticks blank and busy on their wrists,
And hope, with furtive eyes and grappling fists,
Flounders in mud. O Jesus, make it stop!

Base Details

If I were fierce, and bald, and short of breath,
    I'd live with scarlet Majors at the Base,
And speed glum heroes up the line to death.
    You'd see me with my puffy petulant face,
Guzzling and gulping in the best hotel,
    Reading the Roll of Honour. 'Poor young chap,'
I'd say – 'I used to know his father well;
    Yes, we've lost heavily in this last scrap.'
And when the war is done and youth stone dead,
I'd toddle safely home and die – in bed.

The General

'Good-morning, good-morning!' the General said
When we met him last week on our way to the line.
Now the soldiers he smiled at are most of 'em dead,
And we're cursing his staff for incompetent swine.
'He's a cheery old card,' grunted Harry to Jack
As they slogged up to Arras with rifle and pack.

But he did for them both by his plan of attack.

*Sassoon disliked being called simply a war poet but it was his poems about the
Great War, mostly short and sharp like these three, that made him famous. He
campaigned publicly against the war, in which he served with much distinction,
being twice wounded and receiving the Military Cross for gallantry in action.*

Solitude   156

HAROLD MONRO

When you have tidied all things for the night,
And while your thoughts are fading to their sleep,
You'll pause a moment in the late firelight,
Too sorrowful to weep.

The large and gentle furniture has stood
In sympathetic silence all the day
With that old kindness of domestic wood;
Nevertheless the haunted room will say:
'Some one must be away.'

The little dog rolls over half awake,
Stretches his paws, yawns, looking up at you,
Wags his tail very slightly for your sake,
That you may feel he is unhappy too.

A distant engine whistles, or the floor
Creaks, or the wandering night-wind bangs a door.

[continued]

Silence is scattered like a broken glass.
The minutes prick their ears and run about,
Then one by one subside again and pass
Sedately in, monotonously out.

You bend your head and wipe away a tear.
Solitude walks one heavy step more near.

*Well known as a poet in his day, almost forgotten now, Monro was also a
publisher who brought out five important anthologies of Georgian Poetry over
the years 1912–22. This poem of his is straightforward and unspectacular in
the Georgian manner with its portrayal of somebody who has been deserted or
widowed.*

157 When I Have Seen by Time's Fell Hand Defaced

WILLIAM SHAKESPEARE

When I have seen by Time's fell hand defaced
The rich proud cost of outworn buried age;
When sometime lofty towers I see down-razed,
And brass eternal slave to mortal rage;
When I have seen the hungry ocean gain
Advantage on the kingdon of the shore,
And the firm soil win of the watery main,
Increasing store with loss, and loss with store;
When I have seen such interchange of state,
Or state itself confounded to decay,
Ruin hath taught me thus to ruminate,
That Time will come and take my Love away.
⠀⠀⠀This thought is as a death, which cannot choose
⠀⠀⠀But weep to have that which it fears to lose.

*When Shakespeare talked about towers being thrown down and memorial
tablets defaced his meaning was not fanciful. There had been internal battles
and rebellions down to his own day, and England was still an insecure place to
a degree that makes our time look like a golden age of calm. His plays are full
of it.*

To His Mother, C.L.M. 158

JOHN MASEFIELD

In the dark womb where I began
My mother's life made me a man.
Through all the months of human birth
Her beauty fed my common earth.
I cannot see, nor breathe, nor stir,
But through the death of some of her.

Down in the darkness of the grave
She cannot see the life she gave.
For all her love, she cannot tell
Whether I use it ill or well,
Nor knock at dusty doors to find
Her beauty dusty in the mind.

If the grave's gates could be undone,
She would not know her little son,
I am so grown. If we should meet
She would pass by me in the street,
Unless my soul's face let her see
My sense of what she did for me.

What have I done to keep in mind
My debt to her and womankind?
What woman's happier life repays
Her for those months of wretched days?
For all my mouthless body leeched
Ere Birth's releasing hell was reached?

What have I done, or tried, or said
In thanks to that dear woman dead?
Men triumph over women still,
Men trample women's rights at will,
And man's lust roves the world untamed.

. . . .

O grave, keep shut lest I be shamed.

Most of the time, Masefield is a poet of action and the outdoors. This
commemoration to his mother, Caroline Louisa Masefield, is in a very different
style, subdued but strongly felt, ending with an indignant bash at the way men
take women for granted. But note that he was writing over 70 years ago, before
'women's rights' got their capital letters.

One Hard Look

159

ROBERT GRAVES

Small gnats that fly
In hot July
And lodge in sleeping ears,
Can rouse therein
A trumpet's din
With Day of Judgement fears.

Small mice at night
Can wake more fright
Than lions at midday;
A straw can crack
The camel's back –
There is no easier way.

One smile relieves
A heart that grieves
Though deadly sad it be,
And one hard look
Can close the book
That lovers love to see.

This comes from early in Graves's career when he was spoken of as one of the Georgian poets, a group that included Rupert Brooke and John Masefield, and set out to write about ordinary life in a simple, natural way. But already in this 'simple' poem there are hints of the magical strain he was soon to develop and make his own.

The Kingdom of God 160

FRANCIS THOMPSON

O world invisible, we view thee,
O world intangible, we touch thee,
O world unknowable, we know thee,
Inapprehensible, we clutch thee!

Does the fish soar to find the ocean,
The eagle plunge to find the air –
That we ask of the stars in motion
If they have rumour of thee there?

Not where the wheeling systems darken,
And our benumbed conceiving soars! –
The drift of pinions, would we hearken,
Beats at our own clay-shuttered doors.

The angels keep their ancient places; –
Turn but a stone, and start a wing!
'Tis ye, 'tis your estrangèd faces,
That miss the many-splendoured thing.

But (when so sad thou canst not sadder)
Cry; – and upon thy so sore loss
Shall shine the traffic of Jacob's ladder
Pitched betwixt Heaven and Charing Cross.

Yea, in the night, my Soul, my daughter,
Cry, – clinging Heaven by the hems;
And lo, Christ walking on the water
Not of Gennesareth, but Thames!

Thompson was a Roman Catholic and also something of a layabout and drunkard. Much of his verse is unreadable today, but nobody has ever conveyed the message that the Kingdom of God is all around us more stirringly than he does in this poem. 'The many-splendoured thing' – his phrase – is not any usual kind of love but something like the glory of God.

161

Ode on Melancholy

JOHN KEATS

No, no! go not to Lethe, neither twist
    Wolf's-bane, tight-rooted, for its poisonous wine;
Nor suffer thy pale forehead to be kist
    By nightshade, ruby grape of Proserpine;
Make not your rosary of yew-berries,
      Nor let the beetle, nor the death-moth be
        Your mournful Psyche, nor the downy owl
A partner in your sorrow's mysteries;
      For shade to shade will come too drowsily,
        And drown the wakeful anguish of the soul.

But when the melancholy fit shall fall
    Sudden from heaven like a weeping cloud,
That fosters the droop-headed flowers all,
    And hides the green hill in an April shroud;
Then glut thy sorrow on a morning rose,
    Or on the rainbow of the salt sand-wave,
      Or on the wealth of globed peonies;
Or if thy mistress some rich anger shows,
      Emprison her soft hand, and let her rave,
        And feed deep, deep upon her peerless eyes.

She dwells with Beauty – Beauty that must die;
    And Joy, whose hand is ever at his lips
Bidding adieu; and aching Pleasure nigh,
    Turning to poison while the bee-mouth sips:
Ay, in the very temple of Delight
    Veiled Melancholy has her sovran shrine,
      Though seen of none save him whose strenuous tongue
      Can burst Joy's grape against his palate fine;
His soul shall taste the sadness of her might,
      And be among her cloudy trophies hung.

Today Keats is probably valued most highly for his odes, half a dozen not very
long poems that have had more effect on later poetry than anything
comparable. They are full of classical references. In this one, Lethe is a
legendary river producing forgetfulness; Proserpine is queen of the infernal
regions; Psyche is an image of the human soul.

The Way Through the Woods

162

RUDYARD KIPLING

They shut the road through the woods
Seventy years ago.
Weather and rain have undone it again,
And now you would never know
There was once a road through the woods
Before they planted the trees.
It is underneath the coppice and heath
And the thin anemones.
Only the keeper sees
That, where the ring-dove broods,
And the badgers roll at ease,
There was once a road through the woods.

Yet, if you enter the woods
Of a summer evening late,
When the night-air cools on the trout-ringed pools
Where the otter whistles his mate,
(They fear not men in the woods,
Because they see so few)
You will hear the beat of a horse's feet,
And the swish of a skirt in the dew,
Steadily cantering through
The misty solitudes,
As though they perfectly knew
The old lost road through the woods . . .
But there is no road through the woods.

*Kipling's poetry comes in several distinct styles: the vigorous vernacular pieces
about army life, the solemn addresses to the nation in time of war or crisis, the
bustling narratives, and more. This poem is different from any of the others — if
his name were not on it nobody, I think, could guess it was one of his.*

The Rum Tum Tugger

T. S. ELIOT

The Rum Tum Tugger is a Curious Cat:
If you offer him pheasant he would rather have grouse.
If you put him in a house he would much prefer a flat,
If you put him in a flat then he'd rather have a house.
If you set him on a mouse then he only wants a rat,
If you set him on a rat then he'd rather chase a mouse.
Yes the Rum Tum Tugger is a Curious Cat –
   And there isn't any call for me to shout it:
    For he will do
    As he do do
      And there's no doing anything about it!

The Rum Tum Tugger is a terrible bore:
When you let him in, then he wants to be out;
He's always on the wrong side of every door,
And as soon as he's at home, then he'd like to get about.
He likes to lie in the bureau drawer,
But he makes such a fuss if he can't get out.
Yes the Rum Tum Tugger is a Curious Cat –
   And it isn't any use for you to doubt it:
    For he will do
    As he do do
      And there's no doing anything about it!

The Rum Tum Tugger is a curious beast:
His disobliging ways are a matter of habit.
If you offer him fish then he always wants a feast;
When there isn't any fish then he won't eat rabbit.
If you offer him cream then he sniffs and sneers,
For he only likes what he finds for himself;
So you'll catch him in it right up to the ears,
If you put it away on the larder shelf . . .
The Rum Tum Tugger is artful and knowing,
The Rum Tum Tugger doesn't care for a cuddle;
But he'll leap on your lap in the middle of your sewing,
For there's nothing he enjoys like a horrible muddle.

Yes the Rum Tum Tugger is a Curious Cat –
And there isn't any need for me to spout it:
For he will do
As he do do
And there's no doing anything about it!

The sage and serious poet Eliot of The Waste Land *and* Four Quartets
*had a playful and fanciful side which came out in his cat poems, treasured by
connoisseurs of whimsy long before Andrew Lloyd Webber set some of them to
music in* Cats. *I love them, but would hate having to defend them to any sage
or serious person.*

The Roads Also

164

WILFRED OWEN

The roads also have their wistful rest,
When the weathercocks perch still and roost,
And the town is a candle-lit room –
The streets also dream their dream.

The old houses muse of the old days
And their fond trees leaning on them doze,
On their steps chatter and clatter stops,
On their doors a strange hand taps.

Men remember alien ardours
As the dusk unearths old mournful odours.
In the garden unborn child souls wail
And the dead scribble on walls.

Though their own child cry for them in tears,
Women weep but hear no sound upstairs.
They believe in loves they had not lived
And in passion past the reach of the stairs
To the world's towers or stars.

*Most of Owen's poems are about war, specifically the Great War in which he
was killed. But there are others of his, like this fragment, that show the much
gentler kind of poet he might have become had he survived. He uses here, as in
many of his poems, a kind of reverse-rhyme in which the consonants remain the
same but the vowel is changed.*

Of My Dear Son, Gervase Beaumont

165

SIR JOHN BEAUMONT

Can I, who have for others oft compiled
The songs of Death, forget my sweetest child,
Which, like a flower crushed, with a blast is dead,
And ere full time hangs down his smiling head,
Expecting with clear hope to live anew
Among the angels, fed with heavenly dew?
We have this sign of joy, that many days,
While on the earth his struggling spirit stays,
The name of Jesus in his mouth contains
His only food, his sleep, his ease from pains.
O may that sound be rooted in my mind,
Of which in him such strong effect I find.
Dear Lord, receive my son, whose winning love
To me was like a friendship, far above
The course of nature or his tender age,
Whose looks could all my bitter griefs assuage;
Let his pure soul ordained seven years to be
In that frail body, which was part of me,
Remain my pledge in Heaven, as sent to show
How to this port at every step I go.

Beaumont was a prosperous Leicestershire landowner. He wrote a great deal of
verse, including an eight-volume religious work, now lost, but nothing better
than this touchingly personal elegy. In the middle he goes into the present tense
while still writing about the past, which may confuse a modern reader but was
common practice in those days.

Tears, Idle Tears

ALFRED, LORD TENNYSON

Tears, idle tears, I know not what they mean,
Tears from the depth of some divine despair
Rise in the heart, and gather to the eyes,
In looking on the happy autumn-fields,
And thinking of the days that are no more.

Fresh as the first beam glittering on a sail,
That brings our friends up from the underworld,
Sad as the last which reddens over one
That sinks with all we love below the verge;
So sad, so fresh, the days that are no more.

Ah, sad and strange as in dark summer dawns
The earliest pipe of half-awaken'd birds
To dying ears, when unto dying eyes
The casement slowly grows a glimmering square;
So sad, so strange, the days that are no more.

Dear as remember'd kisses after death,
And sweet as those by hopeless fancy feign'd
On lips that are for others; deep as love,
Deep as first love, and wild with all regret;
O Death in Life, the days that are no more!

Tennyson is a poet of many moods and styles, but there can be no doubt that he
is most at home when expressing grief and feelings of loss, as in this poem. He
said of it that he was not thinking of any particular reason for sorrow, more a
general yearning for the past, something he had always felt even as a boy.

Tell Me Not Here

A. E. HOUSMAN

Tell me not here, it needs not saying,
    What tune the enchantress plays
In aftermaths of soft September
    Or under blanching mays,
For she and I were long acquainted
    And I knew all her ways.

On russet floors, by waters idle,
    The pine lets fall its cone;
The cuckoo shouts all day at nothing
    In leafy dells alone;
And traveller's joy beguiles in autumn
    Hearts that have lost their own.

On acres of the seeded grasses
    The changing burnish heaves;
Or marshalled under moons of harvest
    Stand still all night the sheaves;
Or beeches strip in storms for winter
    And stain the wind with leaves.

Possess, as I possessed a season,
    The countries I resign,
Where over elmy plains the highway
    Would mount the hills and shine,
And full of shade the pillared forest
    Would murmur and be mine.

For nature, heartless, witless nature,
    Will neither care nor know
What stranger's feet may find the meadow
    And trespass there and go,
Nor ask amid the dews of morning
    If they are mine or no.

*Housman's way of writing about both God and man may be eccentric and even
tiresome at times, but no poet known to me has surpassed him in his portrayal
of 'the enchantress' Nature. He could find the right brief words for what we
have all seen and not noticed. Traveller's joy is the wild clematis – flowers can
distract the unhappy.*

Ruth

THOMAS HOOD

She stood breast high amid the corn,
Clasp'd by the golden light of morn,
Like the sweetheart of the sun,
Who many a glowing kiss had won.

On her cheek an autumn flush,
Deeply ripened; – such a blush
In the midst of brown was born,
Like red poppies grown with corn.

Round her eyes her tresses fell,
Which were blackest none could tell,
But long lashes veil'd a light,
That had else been all too bright.

And her hat, with shady brim,
Made her tressy forehead dim; –
Thus she stood amid the stooks,
Praising God with sweetest looks:

Sure, I said, heav'n did not mean,
Where I reap thou shouldst but glean,
Lay thy sheaf adown and come,
Share my harvest and my home.

Hood wrote a great many poems in different styles, comic and serious, now and
then concerned with social questions, now and then personal, like this one. His
Ruth owes something to the Ruth of the Old Testament, something perhaps to
the Ruth of Keats's Nightingale ode, but she is very much Hood's own, too.

Dover Beach

MATTHEW ARNOLD

The sea is calm to-night.
The tide is full, the moon lies fair
Upon the straits; – on the French coast, the light
Gleams and is gone; the cliffs of England stand,
Glimmering and vast, out in the tranquil bay.
Come to the window, sweet is the night air!
Only, from the long line of spray
Where the sea meets the moon-blanch'd land,
Listen! you hear the grating roar
Of pebbles which the waves draw back, and fling,
At their return, up the high strand,
Begin, and cease, and then again begin,
With tremulous cadence slow, and bring
The eternal note of sadness in.

Sophocles long ago,
Heard it on the Ægæan, and it brought
Into his mind the turbid ebb and flow
Of human misery; we
Find also in the sound a thought,
Hearing it by this distant northern sea.

The Sea of Faith
Was once, too, at the full, and round earth's shore
Lay like the folds of a bright girdle furl'd;
But now I hear
Its melancholy, long, withdrawing roar,
Retreating, to the breath
Of the night-wind, down the vast edges drear
And naked shingles of the world.

Ah, love, let us be true
To one another! for the world, which seems
To lie before us like a land of dreams,
So various, so beautiful, so new,
Hath really neither joy, nor love, nor light,

Nor certitude, nor peace, nor help for pain;
And we are here as on a darkling plain
Swept with confused alarms of struggle and flight,
Where ignorant armies clash by night.

Arnold was not alone in his time in lamenting the decay of religious faith, but nobody saw more clearly its consequences, the terrible vulnerability of the human race when deprived of that protection. He wrote this poem about 1850, when it must have seemed to many people that Christian belief was still firmly established.

Margaret Love Peacock: For Her Tombstone, 1826

170

THOMAS LOVE PEACOCK

Long night succeeds thy little day;
    Oh blighted blossom! can it be,
That this grey stone and grassy clay
    Have closed our anxious care of thee?

The half-form'd speech of artless thought,
    That spoke a mind beyond thy years;
The song, the dance, by nature taught;
    The sunny smiles, the transient tears;

The symmetry of face and form,
    The eye with light and life replete;
The little heart so fondly warm;
    The voice so musically sweet.

These lost to hope, in memory yet
    Around the hearts that lov'd thee cling,
Shadowing, with long and vain regret,
    The too fair promise of thy spring.

Peacock enjoyed long life and success in two careers, as a poet and novelist and as a chief secretary to the East India Company. He was a close friend of Shelley's. Yet he was heavily hit by bereavement, losing three of his four children. In this poem he laments the death of a daughter at the age of four.

171 An Elegy on That Glory of Her Sex, Mrs Mary Blaize

OLIVER GOLDSMITH

Good people all, with one accord,
  Lament for Madam BLAIZE,
Who never wanted a good word –
  From those who spoke her praise!

The needy seldom pass'd her door,
  And always found her kind;
She freely lent to all the poor, –
  Who left a pledge behind.

She strove the neighbourhood to please,
  With manners wond'rous winning,
And never follow'd wicked ways, –
  Unless when she was sinning.

At church, in silks and sattins new,
  With hoop of monstrous size,
She never slumber'd in her pew, –
  But when she shut her eyes.

Her love was sought, I do aver,
  By twenty beaus and more;
The king himself has follow'd her, –
  When she has walk'd before.

But now her wealth and finery fled,
  Her hanger's-on cut short all;
The doctors found, when she was dead, –
  Her last disorder mortal.

Let us lament, in sorrow sore,
  For Kent-street well may say,
That had she liv'd a twelve-month more,
  She had not dy'd to-day.

Goldsmith, son of an Irish clergyman, was a failed doctor and hack journalist
who was also a playwright and a versatile poet, highly thought of by Dr
Johnson. This light piece is a good-natured skit on the kind of empty
commendatory verses that used at the time to be run up on the death of
anybody of supposed grandeur.

To Autumn

JOHN KEATS

Season of mists and mellow fruitfulness,
    Close bosom-friend of the maturing sun;
Conspiring with him how to load and bless
    With fruit the vines that round the thatch-eves run;
To bend with apples the moss'd cottage-trees,
    And fill all fruit with ripeness to the core;
        To swell the gourd, and plump the hazel shells
    With a sweet kernel; to set budding more,
And still more, later flowers for the bees,
Until they think warm days will never cease,
    For Summer has o'er-brimm'd their clammy cells.

Who hath not seen thee oft amid thy store?
    Sometimes whoever seeks abroad may find
Thee sitting careless on a granary floor,
    Thy hair soft-lifted by the winnowing wind;
Or on a half-reap'd furrow sound asleep,
    Drows'd with the fume of poppies, while thy hook
        Spares the next swath and all its twined flowers:
And sometimes like a gleaner thou dost keep
    Steady thy laden head across a brook;
    Or by a cyder-press, with patient look,
        Thou watchest the last oozings hours by hours.

Where are the songs of Spring? Ay, where are they?
    Think not of them, thou hast thy music too, –
While barred clouds bloom the soft-dying day,
    And touch the stubble-plains with rosy hue;
Then in a wailful choir the small gnats mourn
    Among the river sallows, borne aloft
        Or sinking as the light wind lives or dies;
And full-grown lambs loud bleat from hilly bourn;
    Hedge-crickets sing; and now with treble soft
    The red-breast whistles from a garden croft;
        And gathering swallows twitter in the skies.

This is usually counted as one of Keats's odes, but it differs from the rest and
from much of his other work in having nothing to do with classical gods and
goddesses and such – the sights and sounds are completely English. The middle
verse, with its strange, haunting personification of Autumn, was probably an
afterthought.

173

A Boy's Song

JAMES HOGG

Where the pools are bright and deep,
Where the gray trout lies asleep,
Up the river and o'er the lea,
That's the way for Billy and me.

Where the blackbird sings the latest,
Where the hawthorn blooms the sweetest,
Where the nestlings chirp and flee,
That's the way for Billy and me.

Where the mowers mow the cleanest,
Where the hay lies thick and greenest;
There to trace the homeward bee,
That's the way for Billy and me.

Where the hazel bank is steepest,
Where the shadow falls the deepest,
Where the clustering nuts fall free,
That's the way for Billy and me.

Why the boys should drive away
Little sweet maidens from the play,
Or love to banter and fight so well,
That's the thing I never could tell.

But this I know, I love to play,
Through the meadow, among the hay;
Up the water and o'er the lea,
That's the way for Billy and me.

Hogg was known as the Ettrick Shepherd, having been born in the Ettrick Forest
in southern Scotland and actually having worked as a shepherd before his
poems were discovered by Sir Walter Scott. At that time childhood was a more
or less unexplored literary territory, and the nineteenth century became the
great age of children's books.

Prospice

ROBERT BROWNING

Fear death? – to feel the fog in my throat,
  The mist in my face,
When the snows begin, and the blasts denote
  I am nearing the place,
The power of the night, the press of the storm,
  The post of the foe;
Where he stands, the Arch Fear in a visible form,
  Yet the strong man must go:
For the journey is done and the summit attained,
  And the barriers fall,
Though a battle's to fight ere the guerdon be gained,
  The reward of it all.
I was ever a fighter, so – one fight more,
  The best and the last!
I would hate that death bandaged my eyes, and forbore,
  And bade me creep past.
No! let me taste the whole of it, fare like my peers
  The heroes of old,
Bear the brunt, in a minute pay glad life's arrears
  Of pain, darkness and cold.
For sudden the worst turns the best to the brave,
  The black minute's at end,
And the elements' rage, the fiend-voices that rave,
  Shall dwindle, shall blend,
Shall change, shall become first a peace out of pain,
  Then a light, then thy breast,
O thou soul of my soul! I shall clasp thee again,
  And with God be the rest!

The title is Latin, meaning 'look forward', a phrase that could almost be called Browning's motto, and if anyone ever looked forward to death, saw it as an adventure, it was he. The soul of his soul is his wife, Elizabeth Barrett Browning, who died before her time in 1861. He wrote this poem not long afterwards.

175 # Anthem for Doomed Youth

WILFRED OWEN

What passing-bells for these who die as cattle?
    Only the monstrous anger of the guns.
    Only the stuttering rifles' rapid rattle
Can patter out their hasty orisons.
No mockeries now for them; no prayers nor bells,
    Nor any voice of mourning save the choirs, –
The shrill, demented choirs of wailing shells;
    And bugles calling for them from sad shires.

What candles may be held to speed them all?
    Not in the hands of boys, but in their eyes
Shall shine the holy glimmers of good-byes.
    The pallor of girls' brows shall be their pall;
Their flowers the tenderness of patient minds,
And each slow dusk a drawing-down of blinds.

All Owen's grief and indignation at what he saw on the Western Front in 1917
are concentrated in this sonnet, one of the most powerful war poems ever
written. The last line refers to the custom of pulling down the blinds when there
was a death in the house or when a funeral was passing; so the mourning will
never end.

Rock of Ages

AUGUSTUS MONTAGUE TOPLADY

Rock of ages, cleft for me,
Let me hide myself in thee;
Let the water and the blood,
From thy riven side which flowed,
Be of sin the double cure:
Cleanse me from its guilt and power.

Not the labours of my hands
Can fulfil thy law's demands;
Could my zeal no respite know,
Could my tears for ever flow,
All for sin could not atone:
Thou must save, and thou alone.

Nothing in my hand I bring;
Simply to thy cross I cling;
Naked, come to thee for dress;
Helpless, look to thee for grace;
Foul, I to the fountain fly;
Wash me, Saviour, or I die.

While I draw this fleeting breath,
When mine eyes are closed in death,
When I soar through tracts unknown,
See thee on thy judgment throne;
Rock of ages, cleft for me,
Let me hide myself in thee.

Augustus Montague Toplady, a parson whose surname pleasingly indicates a
womanising ancestor, is supposed to have got the idea for this poem while
sheltering from a storm in a fissure in Cheddar Gorge. More than a century
after its publication, a survey of over 400,000 English hymns gave it a place
among the most popular four.

from
177   The Burning of the Leaves

LAURENCE BINYON

Now is the time for the burning of the leaves.
They go to the fire; the nostril pricks with smoke
Wandering slowly into a weeping mist.
Brittle and blotched, ragged and rotten sheaves!
A flame seizes the smouldering ruin and bites
On stubborn stalks that crackle as they resist.

The last hollyhock's fallen tower is dust;
All the spices of June are a bitter reek,
All the extravagant riches spent and mean.
All burns! The reddest rose is a ghost;
Sparks whirl up, to expire in the mist: the wild
Fingers of fire are making corruption clean.

Now is the time for stripping the spirit bare,
Time for the burning of days ended and done,
Idle solace of things that have gone before:
Rootless hopes and fruitless desire are there;
Let them go to the fire, with never a look behind.
The world that was ours is a world that is ours no more.

They will come again, the leaf and the flower, to arise
From squalor of rottenness into the old splendour,
And magical scents to a wondering memory bring;
The same glory, to shine upon different eyes.
Earth cares for her own ruins, naught for ours.
Nothing is certain, only the certain spring.

In the first half of this extract Binyon carefully sets the scene with a close
description of the bonfire – not forgetting the sounds and smells and smoke in
the eyes. Having done so he reflects that though the cycle of the seasons is
permanent we are not part of it and, unlike the leaves, are not ever-renewed.

A Child Ill

SIR JOHN BETJEMAN

Oh, little body, do not die.
    The soul looks out through wide blue eyes
So questioningly into mine,
    That my tormented soul replies:

'Oh, little body, do not die.
    You hold the soul that talks to me
Although our conversation be
    As wordless as the windy sky.'

So looked my father at the last
    Right in my soul, before he died,
Though words we spoke went heedless past
    As London traffic-roar outside.

And now the same blue eyes I see
    Look through me from a little son,
So questioning, so searchingly
    That youthfulness and age are one.

My father looked at me and died
    Before my soul made full reply.
Lord, leave this other Light alight –
    Oh, little body, do not die.

There are some poems on which any comment would be an intrusion.
This is one.

Fidele's Dirge

179

WILLIAM SHAKESPEARE

Fear no more the heat o' the sun,
    Nor the furious winter's rages;
Thou thy worldly task hast done,
    Home art gone, and ta'en thy wages.
Golden lads and girls all must,
As chimney-sweepers, come to dust.

Fear no more the frown o' the great,
    Thou art past the tyrant's stroke;
Care no more to clothe and eat,
    To thee the reed is as the oak.
The sceptre, learning, physic, must
All follow this, and come to dust.

Fear no more the lightning-flash,
    Nor the all-dreaded thunder-stone;
Fear not slander, censure rash;
    Thou hast finished joy and moan.
All lovers young, all lovers must
Consign to thee, and come to dust.

No exorciser harm thee!
Nor no witchcraft charm thee!
Ghost unlaid forbear thee!
Nothing ill come near thee!
Quiet consummation have,
And renowned by thy grave!

Elizabethan plays, especially comedies, were often diversified by songs. Most of Shakespeare's are not just pleasant material for music but short poems full of meaning and atmosphere, often mysterious or magical. Cymbeline, from which this one is taken, is a comedy in the happy-ever-after tradition, and so Fidele turns out not to be dead after all.

The Long Small Room

EDWARD THOMAS

The long small room that showed willows in the west
Narrowed up to the end the fireplace filled,
Although not wide. I liked it. No one guessed
What need or accident made them so build.

Only the moon, the mouse and the sparrow peeped
In from the ivy round the casement thick.
Of all they saw and heard there they shall keep
The tale for the old ivy and older brick.

When I look back I am like moon, sparrow and mouse
That witnessed what they could never understand
Or alter or prevent in the dark house.
One thing remains the same – this my right hand.

Crawling crab-like over the clean white page,
Resting awhile each morning on the pillow,
Then once more starting to crawl on towards age.
The hundred last leaves stream upon the willow.

This is the first of Thomas's poems I ever read. It impressed me as being like someone talking to me directly, seriously and honestly. I see now more than before, perhaps, the force of his gentle reminder that we have no power over the world around us and merely 'crawl on towards age' as the seasons pass.

1887

A. E. HOUSMAN

From Clee to heaven the beacon burns,
  The shires have seen it plain,
From north and south the sign returns
  And beacons burn again.

Look left, look right, the hills are bright,
  The dales are light between,
Because 'tis fifty years to-night
  That God has saved the Queen.

Now, when the flame they watch not towers
  About the soil they trod,
Lads, we'll remember friends of ours
  Who shared the work with God.

To skies that knit their heartstrings right,
  To fields that bred them brave,
The saviours come not home to-night:
  Themselves they could not save.

It dawns in Asia, tombstones show
  And Shropshire names are read;
And the Nile spills his overflow
  Beside the Severn's dead.

We pledge in peace by farm and town
  The Queen they served in war,
And fire the beacons up and down
  The land they perished for.

'God save the Queen' we living sing,
  From height to height 'tis heard;
And with the rest your voices ring,
  Lads of the Fifty-third.

Oh, God will save her, fear you not:
  Be you the men you've been,
Get you the sons your fathers got,
  And God will save the Queen.

This first poem in Housman's first collection, A Shropshire Lad, was
written to commemorate Queen Victoria's Golden Jubilee. It is patriotic, but
not unthinkingly so, in its recognition that the nation is preserved by the deaths
of private soldiers. (The 53rd Regiment of Foot was raised in Shropshire and
later formed part of the King's Shropshire Light Infantry.)

Jack and Joan

THOMAS CAMPION

Jack and Joan they think no ill,
But loving live, and merry still;
Do their week-days' work, and pray
Devoutly on the holy day;
Skip and trip it on the green,
And help to choose the Summer Queen;
Lash out at a country feast
Their silver penny with the best.

Well can they judge of nappy ale,
And tell at large a winter tale;
Climb up to the apple loft,
And turn the crabs till they be soft.
Tib is all the father's joy,
And little Tom the mother's boy.
All their pleasure is content,
And care to pay their yearly rent.

Joan can call by name her cows,
And deck her windows with green boughs;
She can wreaths and tutties make,
And trim with plums a bridal cake.
Jack knows what brings gain or loss,
And his long flail can stoutly toss;
Make the hedge which others break,
And ever thinks what he doth speak.

Now you courtly dames and knights,
That study only strange delights,
Though you scorn the home-spun gray
And revel in your rich array;
Though your tongues dissemble deep
And can your heads from danger keep:
Yet for all your pomp and train,
Securer lives the silly swain.

Campion was a composer as well as a poet, writing both words and music of
many songs and madrigals. He also studied law, fought in France under the
Earl of Essex and practised as a 'doctor in phisicke'. More perhaps than some
who have used the theme, he earned the right to the envy of a simple rural life
expressed here. (A 'silly swain' was an innocent rustic.)

183 # 1805

ROBERT GRAVES

At Viscount Nelson's lavish funeral,
   While the mob milled and yelled about St Paul's
A General chatted with an Admiral:

'One of your Colleagues, Sir, remarked today
   That Nelson's exit, though to be lamented,
Falls not inopportunely, in its way.'

'He was a thorn in our flesh,' came the reply –
   'The most bird-witted, unaccountable,
Odd little runt that ever I did spy.

'One arm, one peeper, vain as Pretty Poll,
   A meddler, too, in foreign politics
And gave his heart in pawn to a plain moll.

'He would dare lecture us Sea Lords, and then
   Would treat his ratings as though men of honour
And play at leap-frog with his midshipmen!

'We tried to box him down, but up he popped,
   And when he'd banged Napoleon at the Nile
Became too much the hero to be dropped.

'You've heard that Copenhagen "blind eye" story?
   We'd tied him to Nurse Parker's apron-strings –
By G–d, he snipped them through and snatched the glory!'

'Yet,' cried the General, 'six-and-twenty sail
   Captured or sunk by him off Tráfalgár –
That writes a handsome finis to the tale.'

'Handsome enough. The seas are England's now.
   That fellow's foibles need no longer plague us.
He died most creditably, I'll allow.'

'And, Sir, the secret of his victories?'
   'By his unServicelike, familiar ways, Sir,
He made the whole Fleet love him, damn his eyes!'

The Battle of Trafalgar, at which a British fleet under Lord Nelson defeated a
combined French and Spanish fleet, took place on 21 October, 1805. The final
verdict of Graves's admiral is close to the mark, though he could have added,
'and the whole country, too.' Nelson was a national hero on a scale
unimaginable today.

from
In Memoriam

ALFRED, LORD TENNYSON

Calm is the morn without a sound,
　　Calm as to suit a calmer grief,
　　And only through the faded leaf
The chestnut pattering to the ground:

Calm and deep peace on this light wold,
　　And on these dews that drench the furze,
　　And all the silvery gossamers
That twinkle into green and gold:

Calm and still light on yon great plain
　　That sweeps with all its autumn bowers,
　　And crowded farms and lessening towers,
To mingle with the bounding main:

Calm and deep peace in this wide air,
　　These leaves that redden to the fall;
　　And in my heart, if calm at all,
If any calm, a calm despair:

Calm on the seas, and silver sleep,
　　And waves that sway themselves in rest,
　　And dead calm in that noble breast
Which heaves but with the heaving deep.

*Tennyson jotted down his greatest poem over the years in 'a thing like a
butcher's account book' with no thought of publication. Once he left it behind
in some lodgings and it was only rescued by luck. This extract shows his
characteristic power of choosing physical details that illustrate the emotion he is
writing about.*

185 # Song from Summer's Last Will and Testament

THOMAS NASHE

Adieu, farewell earth's bliss,
This world uncertain is;
Fond are life's lustful joys,
Death proves them all but toys,
None from his darts can fly.
I am sick, I must die.
    Lord have mercy on us!

Rich men, trust not in wealth,
Gold cannot buy you health;
Physic himself must fade,
All things to end are made.
The plague full swift goes by.
I am sick, I must die.
    Lord, have mercy on us!

Beauty is but a flower
Which wrinkles will devour;
Brightness falls from the air,
Queens have died young and fair,
Dust hath closed Helen's eye.
I am sick, I must die.
    Lord, have mercy on us!

Strength stoops unto the grave,
Worms feed on Hector brave,
Swords may not fight with fate,
Earth still holds ope her gate.
Come! Come! The bells do cry.
I am sick, I must die.
    Lord, have mercy on us!

. . . .

Haste, therefore, each degree,
To welcome destiny.
Heaven is our heritage,
Earth but a player's stage;
Mount we unto the sky.
I am sick, I must die.
          Lord, have mercy on us!

Nashe, born in Lowestoft, was a poet, playwright and pamphleteer. Bubonic plague in England and elsewhere had died down since the Black Death of the fourteenth century, but it had never disappeared, and any winter might bring an outbreak. Degree refers to social status; like a true Elizabethan, Nashe emphasises the classlessness of death.

London under Bombardment   186

GRETA BRIGGS

I, who am known as London, have faced stern times before,
Having fought and ruled and traded for a thousand years and more;
I knew the Roman legions and the harsh-voiced Danish hordes;
I heard the Saxon revels, saw blood on the Norman swords.
But, though I am scarred by battle, my grim defenders vow
Never was I so stately nor so well-beloved as now.
The lights that burn and glitter in the exile's lonely dream,
The lights of Piccadilly, and those that used to gleam
Down Regent Street and Kingsway may now no longer shine,
But other lights keep burning, and their splendour, too, is mine,
Seen in the work-worn faces and glimpsed in the steadfast eyes
When little homes lie broken and death descends from the skies.
The bombs have shattered my churches, have torn my streets apart,
But they have not bent my spirit and they shall not break my heart.
For my people's faith and courage are lights of London town
Which still would shine in legends though my last broad bridge were down.

I found this poem, whose author I cannot trace, in Field-Marshal Wavell's fine collection, Other Men's Flowers. He said he came across it in an Egyptian newspaper in 1941 while flying to deal with a dangerous German attack, and 'reading this poem and committing it to memory did something to relieve my discomforts of body and mind.'

Fancy's Knell

A. E. HOUSMAN

When lads were home from labour
  At Abdon under Clee,
A man would call his neighbour
  And both would send for me.
And where the light in lances
  Across the mead was laid,
There to the dances
  I fetched my flute and played.

Ours were idle pleasures,
  Yet oh, content we were,
The young to wind the measures,
  The old to heed the air;
And I to lift with playing
  From tree and tower and steep
The light delaying,
  And flute the sun to sleep.

The youth toward his fancy
  Would turn his brow of tan,
And Tom would pair with Nancy
  And Dick step off with Fan;
The girl would lift her glances
  To his, and both be mute:
Well went the dances
  At evening to the flute.

Wenlock Edge was umbered,
  And bright was Abdon Burf,
And warm between them slumbered
  The smooth green miles of turf;
Until from grass and clover
  The upshot beam would fade,
And England over
  Advanced the lofty shade.

The lofty shade advances,
    I fetch my flute and play:
Come, lads, and learn the dances
    And praise the tune to-day.
To-morrow, more's the pity,
    Away we both must hie,
To air the ditty,
    And to earth I.

This is the last poem in Last Poems, the second of the two collections published in Housman's lifetime. Like the title of the volume, the title of this poem indicates a farewell to the 'fancy' or imagination or poetry. The story told here is entirely fictional, a kind of allegory, but handled with amazing power.

The Lake Isle of Innisfree   188

W. B. YEATS

I will arise and go now, and go to Innisfree,
And a small cabin build there, of clay and wattles made:
Nine bean-rows will I have there, a hive for the honey-bee,
And live alone in the bee-loud glade.

And I shall have some peace there, for peace comes dropping slow,
Dropping from the veils of the morning to where the cricket sings;
There midnight's all a glimmer, and noon a purple glow,
And evening full of the linnet's wings.

I will arise and go now, for always night and day
I hear lake water lapping with low sounds by the shore;
While I stand on the roadway, or on the pavements grey,
I hear it in the deep heart's core.

William Butler Yeats studied art in his youth and worked for the creation of an Irish national theatre, but he is best known for his lyric poems, of which this is the most famous. Some people have considered it affected or insincere, perhaps unaware that Yeats himself considered it to be among the most characteristic of his early works.

The Road

JAMES STEPHENS

Because our lives are cowardly and sly,
 Because we do not dare to take or give,
Because we scowl and pass each other by,
 We do not live; we do not dare to live.

We dive, each man, into his secret house,
 And bolt the door, and listen in affright,
Each timid man beside a timid spouse,
 With timid children huddled out of sight.

Kissing in secret, fighting secretly!
 We crawl and hide like vermin in a hole,
Under the bravery of sun and sky
 We flash our meannesses of face and soul.

Let us go out and walk upon the road,
 And quit for evermore the brick-built den,
The lock and key, the hidden, shy abode
 That separates us from our fellow men.

And by contagion of the sun we may
 Catch at a spark from that primeval fire,
And learn that we are better than our clay,
 And equal to the peaks of our desire.

Stephens was a Dubliner, an active Irish nationalist and a writer of fairy stories based on Irish folk-lore. Some of his poems are more down-to-earth, like this one with its harsh picture of the dreariness of day-to-day urban life. He is more convincing on this than the remedy he proposes, which seems sadly out of reach.

Margaritæ Sorori, I.M. 190

W. E. HENLEY

A late lark twitters from the quiet skies;
And from the west,
Where the sun, his day's work ended,
Lingers as in content,
There falls on the old, gray city
An influence luminous and serene,
A shining peace.

The smoke ascends
In a rosy-and-golden haze. The spires
Shine, and are changed. In the valley
Shadows rise. The lark sings on. The sun,
Closing his benediction,
Sinks, and the darkening air
Thrills with a sense of the triumphing night –
Night, with her train of stars
And her great gift of sleep.

So be my passing!
My task accomplished and the long day done,
My wages taken, and in my heart
Some late lark singing,
Let me be gathered to the quiet west,
The sundown splendid and serene,
Death.

William Ernest Henley addresses this poem to his sister Margaret, in
memoriam. Dating from 1876, it is one of the very first attempts at free verse in
English poetry. On the face of it the poet is asking for a peaceful death, but he
can also be taken as pleading for a full span of life – he was never strong. It was
not to be.

Recessional

191

RUDYARD KIPLING

God of our fathers, known of old,
    Lord of our far-flung battle-line,
Beneath whose awful Hand we hold
    Dominion over palm and pine –
Lord God of Hosts, be with us yet,
Lest we forget – lest we forget!

The tumult and the shouting dies;
    The Captains and the Kings depart:
Still stands Thine ancient sacrifice,
    An humble and a contrite heart.
Lord God of Hosts, be with us yet,
Lest we forget – lest we forget!

Far-call'd, our navies melt away;
    On dune and headland sinks the fire:
Lo, all our pomp of yesterday
    Is one with Nineveh and Tyre!
Judge of the Nations, spare us yet,
Lest we forget – lest we forget!

If, drunk with sight of power, we loose
    Wild tongues that have not Thee in awe,
Such boastings as the Gentiles use,
    Or lesser breeds without the Law –
Lord God of Hosts, be with us yet,
Lest we forget – lest we forget!

For heathen heart that puts her trust
    In reeking tube and iron shard,
All valiant dust that builds on dust,
    And, guarding, calls not Thee to guard –
For frantic boast and foolish word –
Thy Mercy on Thy People, Lord!

Kipling published this famous poem to mark Queen Victoria's Diamond
Jubilee. It is deeply patriotic though not bumptious. On the contrary, it warns
Britain at the height of her Empire to go cautiously, to behave with moderation,
not to be 'drunk with sight of power' or forget her responsibilities under God.
The 'Gentiles' in this context are heathens, foreigners.

The Three Fishers

CHARLES KINGSLEY

Three fishers went sailing away to the West,
　　Away to the West as the sun went down;
Each thought on the woman who loved him the best,
　　And the children stood watching them out of the town;
For men must work, and women must weep,
And there's little to earn, and many to keep,
　　Though the harbour bar be moaning.

Three wives sat up in the lighthouse tower,
　　And they trimmed the lamps as the sun went down;
They looked at the squall, and they looked at the shower,
　　And the night-rack came rolling up ragged and brown.
But men must work, and women must weep,
Though storms be sudden, and waters deep,
　　And the harbour bar be moaning.

Three corpses lay out on the shining sands
　　In the morning gleam as the tide went down,
And the women are weeping and wringing their hands
　　For those who will never come home to the town;
For men must work, and women must weep,
And the sooner it's over, the sooner to sleep;
　　And good-bye to the bar and its moaning.

Kingsley was brought up partly in Clovelly on the North Devon coast and the vivid impression the place made on him is reflected in his work, not least in this poem. For all its briskness of metre this turns out to be a most solemn affair, a meditation on the unchangeable conditions of human life and death.

In Westminster Abbey

193

SIR JOHN BETJEMAN

Let me take this other glove off
　　As the *vox humana* swells,
And the beauteous fields of Eden
　　Bask beneath the Abbey bells.
Here, where England's statesmen lie,
Listen to a lady's cry.

Gracious Lord, oh bomb the Germans.
　　Spare their women for Thy Sake,
And if that is not too easy
　　We will pardon Thy Mistake.
But, gracious Lord, whate'er shall be,
Don't let anyone bomb me.

Keep our Empire undismembered
　　Guide our Forces by Thy Hand,
Gallant blacks from far Jamaica,
　　Honduras and Togoland;
Protect them Lord in all their fights,
And, even more, protect the whites.

Think of what our Nation stands for,
　　Books from Boots' and country lanes,
Free speech, free passes, class distinction,
　　Democracy and proper drains.
Lord, put beneath Thy special care
One-eighty-nine Cadogan Square.

Although dear Lord I am a sinner,
　　I have done no major crime;
Now I'll come to Evening Service
　　Whensoever I have the time.
So, Lord, reserve for me a crown,
And do not let my shares go down.

I will labour for Thy Kingdom,
　　Help our lads to win the war,
Send white feathers to the cowards
　　Join the Women's Army Corps,
Then wash the steps around Thy Throne
In the Eternal Safety Zone.

Now I feel a little better,
What a treat to hear Thy Word,
Where the bones of leading statesmen
Have so often been interr'd.
And now, dear Lord, I cannot wait
Because I have a luncheon date.

There is an invigorating streak of malice in Betjeman's work that occasionally comes to the surface, as in this poem, which dates from early in the last war. Its splendidly detailed portrait of a complacent hypocrite is one any novelist might envy. Strangely, we end with a horrible feeling that the lady is no worse than most of us.

Ozymandias 194

PERCY BYSSHE SHELLEY

I met a traveller from an antique land
Who said: Two vast and trunkless legs of stone
Stand in the desert... Near them, on the sand,
Half sunk, a shattered visage lies, whose frown,
And wrinkled lip, and sneer of cold command,
Tell that its sculptor well those passions read
Which yet survive, stamped on these lifeless things,
The hand that mocked them, and the heart that fed:
And on the pedestal these words appear:
'My name is Ozymandias, king of kings:
Look on my works, ye Mighty, and despair!'
Nothing beside remains. Round the decay
Of that colossal wreck, boundless and bare
The lone and level sands stretch far away.

Nobody has ever written about the emptiness and futility of human power in a more concentrated, telling way than Shelley did in this sonnet. He may have been thinking of Rameses II, King of Egypt in the thirteenth century BC, who put up a 90-foot statue to himself, the largest structure of its kind in the world.

The Guest

ANONYMOUS

Yet if His Majesty, our sovereign lord,
Should of his own accord
Friendly himself invite,
And say 'I'll be your guest to-morrow night,'
How should we stir ourselves, call and command
All hands to work! 'Let no man idle stand!
'Set me fine Spanish tables in the hall;
See they be fitted all;
Let there be room to eat
And order taken that there want no meat.
See every sconce and candlestick made bright,
That without tapers they may give a light.
'Look to the presence: are the carpets spread,
The dazie o'er the head,
The cushions in the chairs,
And all the candles lighted on the stairs?
Perfume the chambers, and in any case
Let each man give attendance in his place!'
Thus, if the king were coming, would we do;
And 'twere good reason too;
For 'tis a duteous thing
To show all honour to an earthly king,
And after all our travail and our cost,
So he be pleased, to think no labour lost.
But at the coming of the King of Heaven
All's set at six and seven;
We wallow in our sin,
Christ cannot find a chamber in the inn.
We entertain him always like a stranger,
And, as at first, still lodge him in the manger.

At the time when this poem was written it was no rare thing for a rich man to
find, not always with much pleasure, that the king had invited himself to dine
and stay the night, or longer, with all his retinue. The contract of such a visit
with an imagined one from Christ is made the sharper by all the realistic detail.
The 'presence' or presence-chamber would be the room for the king to receive
those in attendance and a 'dazie' was a canopy over a chair of state.

Now Sleeps the Crimson Petal 196

ALFRED, LORD TENNYSON

Now sleeps the crimson petal, now the white;
Nor waves the cypress in the palace walk;
Nor winks the gold fin in the porphyry font:
The fire-fly wakens: waken thou with me.

Now droops the milkwhite peacock like a ghost,
And like a ghost she glimmers on to me.

Now like the Earth all Danaë to the stars,
And all thy heart lies open unto me.

Now slides the silent meteor on, and leaves
A shining furrow, as thy thoughts in me.

Now folds the lily all her sweetness up,
And slips into the bosom of the lake:
So fold thyself, my dearest, thou, and slip
Into my bosom and be lost in me.

This lyric has an Eastern flavour and is (very thinly) based on Persian love
poetry. However, line seven takes us into classical mythology. Danaë was a
Greek princess whose father determined she should never marry and shut her up
in a tower. Zeus entered it by temporarily turning himself into a shower of gold
and ravished her. This is used for a bold, almost far-fetched metaphor,
unexpected in Tennyson.

Why So Pale and Wan, Fond Lover?

197

SIR JOHN SUCKLING

Why so pale and wan, fond lover?
Prithee, why so pale?
Will, when looking well can't move her,
Looking ill prevail?
Prithee, why so pale?

Why so dull and mute, young sinner?
Prithee, why so mute?
Will, when speaking well can't win her,
Saying nothing do 't?
Prithee, why so mute?

Quit, quit for shame! This will not move;
This will not take her.
If of herself she will not love,
Nothing can make her:
The devil take her!

Suckling wrote a number of plays and poems but his short life was largely one
of extravagance and adventure. He was a leader of the Royalist party, had to
flee abroad and later committed suicide in Paris for fear of poverty. Handsome,
witty and, until his last days, rich, he was the greatest gambler and card-player
of his time and invented the game of cribbage. With 'fond' he is calling the
lover something like besotted rather than affectionate.

A Short Song of Congratulation 198

SAMUEL JOHNSON

Long-expected one-and-twenty,
Lingering year at last is flown;
Pomp and pleasure, pride and plenty,
Great Sir John, are all your own.

Loosened from the minor's tether,
Free to mortgage or to sell,
Wild as wind, and light as feather,
Bid the slaves of thrift farewell.

Call the Betties, Kates, and Jennies,
Every name that laughs at care;
Lavish of your grandsire's guineas,
Show the spirit of an heir.

All that prey on vice and folly
Joy to see their quarry fly;
Here the gamester light and jolly,
There the lender grave and sly.

Wealth, Sir John, was made to wander,
Let it wander as it will;
See the jockey, see the pander,
Bid them come and take their fill.

When the bonny blade carouses,
Pockets full, and spirits high,
What are acres? What are houses?
Only dirt, or wet or dry.

If the guardian or the mother
Tell the woes of wilful waste,
Scorn their counsel and their pother:
You can hang or drown at last!

This deceptively light-sounding poem is actually quite a bitter attack on the
reckless extravagance so likely to be shown by a young man coming into a large
estate. Johnson writes not out of condemnation of great wealth or envy of it, but
as a solid Tory, indignant at the abdication of duty and responsibility.

Taller Today

W. H. AUDEN

Taller to-day, we remember similar evenings,
Walking together in the windless orchard
Where the brook runs over the gravel, far from the glacier.

Again in the room with the sofa hiding the grate,
Look down to the river when the rain is over,
See him turn to the window, hearing our last
Of Captain Ferguson.

It is seen how excellent hands have turned to commonness.
One staring too long, went blind in a tower,
One sold all his manors to fight, broke through, and faltered.

Nights come bringing the snow, and the dead howl
Under the headlands in their windy dwelling
Because the Adversary put too easy questions
On lonely roads.

But happy now, though no nearer each other,
We see the farms lighted all along the valley;
Down at the mill-shed the hammering stops
And men go home.

Noises at dawn will bring
Freedom for some, but not this peace
No bird can contradict: passing, but is sufficient now
For something fulfilled this hour, loved or endured.

As a leading poet of his generation Wystan Hugh Auden was almost bound to write obscurely at times. If not overdone this can produce an effective mysteriousness, as here with the unknown Captain Ferguson. The last two verses however are clear and impressive enough. (This is the original 1930 version, not the later, cut one.)

Hymn to Diana

BEN JONSON

Queen and huntress, chaste and fair,
　　Now the sun is laid to sleep,
Seated in thy silver chair,
　　　State in wonted manner keep:
　　　　Hesperus entreats thy light,
　　　　Goddess excellently bright.

Earth, let not thy envious shade
　　Dare itself to interpose;
Cynthia's shining orb was made
　　　Heaven to clear when day did close:
　　　　Bless us then with wishèd sight,
　　　　Goddess excellently bright.

Lay thy bow of pearl apart,
　　And thy crystal-shining quiver;
Give unto the flying hart
　　　Space to breathe, how short soever:
　　　　Thou that mak'st a day of night –
　　　　Goddess excellently bright.

This poem is taken from a comedy, Cynthia's Revels, first performed in
1600. The character of Cynthia represented Queen Elizabeth I. Diana and
Cynthia are names for the same Roman moon-goddess, traditionally 'chaste'
like the Virgin Queen. This famous lyric is the only part of the play that is still
remembered.

201

In the Valley of the Elwy

GERARD MANLEY HOPKINS

I remember a house where all were good
    To me, God knows, deserving no such thing:
    Comforting smell breathed at very entering,
Fetched fresh, as I suppose, off some sweet wood.

That cordial air made those kind people a hood
    All over, as a bevy of eggs the mothering wing
    Will, or mild nights the new morsels of Spring:
Why, it seemed of course; seemed of right it should.

Lovely the woods, waters, meadows, combes, vales,
All the air things wear that build this world of Wales;
    Only the inmate does not correspond:

God, lover of souls, swaying considerate scales,
Complete thy creature dear O where it fails,
    Being mighty a master, being a father and fond.

*Gerard Manley Hopkins was a Jesuit priest of such a strict conscience that he
allowed none of his poems to be published in his lifetime. They are
revolutionary in style and their phrasing often runs against English idiom. Here
he is comparatively restrained. Despite the setting of this sonnet and his Welsh
surname, he seems to have had no personal connections with Wales.*

202

Cargoes

JOHN MASEFIELD

Quinquireme of Nineveh from distant Ophir
Rowing home to haven in sunny Palestine,
With a cargo of ivory,
And apes and peacocks,
Sandalwood, cedarwood, and sweet white wine.

Stately Spanish galleon coming from the Isthmus,
Dipping through the Tropics by the palm-green shores,
With a cargo of diamonds,
Emeralds, amethysts,
Topazes, and cinnamon, and gold moidores.

Dirty British coaster with a salt-caked smoke stack
Butting through the channel in the mad March days,
With a cargo of Tyne coal,
Road-rail, pig-lead,
Firewood, iron-ware, and cheap tin trays.

*For many years this poem by a sometime Poet Laureate – he held the post from
1930 until his death – was a favourite anthology and recitation piece. Robert
Graves once unkindly suggested that, since the quinquireme and the galleon
were loaded with stuff easily obtainable at home, the destination of the coaster
with its coal was obviously Newcastle.*

Stopping by Woods on a Snowy Evening

203

ROBERT FROST

Whose woods these are I think I know.
His house is in the village though;
He will not see me stopping here
To watch his woods fill up with snow.

My little horse must think it queer
To stop without a farmhouse near
Between the woods and frozen lake
The darkest evening of the year.

He gives his harness bells a shake
To ask if there is some mistake.
The only other sound's the sweep
Of easy wind and downy flake.

The woods are lovely, dark and deep.
But I have promises to keep
And miles to go before I sleep,
And miles to go before I sleep.

*Born in San Francisco, Frost lived most of his life in New England and wrote
largely about everyday country life there. Almost alone among American poets
of his time he paid no attention to the Modernist movement. He is supposed to
have said that writing poetry without rhyming was like playing tennis without
a net.*

from
204 The Rubáiyát of Omar Khayyám

EDWARD FITZGERALD

Oh, come with old Khayyám and leave the Wise
To talk; one thing is certain, that Life flies;
      One thing is certain, and the Rest is Lies;
The Flower that once has blown for ever dies.

Myself when young did eagerly frequent
Doctor and Saint, and heard great Argument
      About it and about: but evermore
Came out by the same Door as in I went.

With them the Seed of Wisdom did I sow,
And with my own hand labour'd it to grow:
      And this was all the Harvest that I reap'd –
'I came like Water, and like Wind I go.'

Into this Universe, and why not knowing,
Nor whence, like Water willy-nilly flowing:
      And out of it, as Wind along the Waste,
I know not whither, willy-nilly blowing.

'Tis all a Chequer-board of Nights and Days
Where Destiny with Men for Pieces plays:
      Hither and thither moves, and mates, and slays,
And one by one back in the Closet lays.

The Ball no Question makes of Ayes and Noes.
But Right or Left, as strikes the Player goes;
      And He that toss'd Thee down into a Field,
He knows about it all – He knows – He knows!

The Moving Finger writes; and having writ,
Moves on: nor all thy Piety nor Wit
      Shall lure it back to cancel half a Line,
Nor all thy Tears wash out a Word of it.

And that inverted Bowl we call The Sky,
Whereunder crawling coop't we live and die,
      Lift not thy hands to It for help – for It
Rolls impotently on as Thou or I.

Here is a further extract from FitzGerald's adaptation of the medieval Persian
original. The view of life put forward has been described as 'rather smart and
shallow'. Maybe, but it is a view that appeals to most people now and then, if
only for two minutes at a time, and it is presented with great eloquence.

On First Looking into Chapman's Homer

JOHN KEATS

Much have I travell'd in the realms of gold,
  And many goodly states and kingdoms seen;
  Round many western islands have I been
Which bards in fealty to Apollo hold.
Oft of one wide expanse had I been told
  That deep-brow'd Homer ruled as his demesne:
  Yet did I never breathe its pure serene
Till I heard Chapman speak out loud and bold:
Then felt I like some watcher of the skies
  When a new planet swims into his ken;
Or like stout Cortez when with eagle eyes
  He star'd at the Pacific – and all his men
Look'd at each other with a wild surmise –
  Silent, upon a peak in Darien.

Keats was greatly attracted by the mythology and literature of ancient Greece, but he was ignorant of the language and lacked any contact with the works of Homer until he picked up the translation made by George Chapman a couple of hundred years before his time – hence this sonnet. By 'the realms of gold' he means the world of the imagination.

206 My Mistress' Eyes Are Nothing Like the Sun

WILLIAM SHAKESPEARE

My mistress' eyes are nothing like the sun,
Coral is far more red than her lips' red,
If snow be white, why then her breasts are dun,
If hairs be wires, black wires grow on her head,
I have seen roses damask'd, red and white,
But no such roses see I in her cheeks,
And in some perfumes is there more delight
Than in the breath that from my mistress reeks.
I love to hear her speak, yet well I know
That music hath a far more pleasing sound,
I grant I never saw a goddess go,
My mistress, when she walks, treads on the ground.
    And yet, by heaven, I think my love as rare
    As any she belied with false compare.

By an old tradition, still prevalent in Shakespeare's time, a poet would write about his lady's beauty in fulsome terms, giving her eyes brighter than the sun, a bosom whiter than snow, etc. Here that convention gets its comeuppance, but a serious point is made too. In the last line she=woman; compare=comparison.

All Things Bright and Beautiful 207

CECIL FRANCES ALEXANDER

All things bright and beautiful,
  All creatures great and small,
All things wise and wonderful,
  The Lord God made them all.

Each little flower that opens,
  Each little bird that sings,
He made their glowing colours,
  He made their tiny wings.

The purple-headed mountain,
  The river running by,
The sunset and the morning,
  That brightens up the sky:

The cold wind in the winter,
  The pleasant summer sun,
The ripe fruits in the garden,
  He made them every one.

The tall trees in the greenwood,
  The meadows for our play,
The rushes by the water
  To gather every day:

He gave us eyes to see them,
  And lips that we might tell
How great is God Almighty,
  Who has made all things well.

This was originally a children's hymn, but it has always had a wider appeal
than that, presumably because of the enviably optimistic way it confines itself
to the splendid or at least agreeable parts of the creation. Not that an educated
Victorian like Mrs Alexander would have thought she was telling the whole
story.

The Rolling English Road

G. K. CHESTERTON

Before the Roman came to Rye or out to Severn strode,
The rolling English drunkard made the rolling English road,
A reeling road, a rolling road, that rambles round the shire,
And after him a parson ran, the sexton and the squire;
A merry road, a mazy road, and such as we did tread
The night we went to Birmingham by way of Beachy Head.

I knew no harm of Bonaparte and plenty of the Squire,
And for to fight the Frenchmen I did not much desire;
But I did bash their baggonets because they came arrayed
To straighten out the crooked road an English drunkard made,
Where you and I went down the lane with ale-mugs in our hands,
The night we went to Glastonbury by way of Goodwin Sands.

His sins they were forgiven him; or why do flowers run
Behind him; and the hedges all strengthening in the sun?
The wild thing went from left to right and knew not which was which,
But the wild rose was above him when they found him in the ditch.
God pardon us, nor harden us; we did not see so clear
The night we went to Bannockburn by way of Brighton Pier.

My friends, we will not go again or ape an ancient rage,
Or stretch the folly of our youth to be the shame of age,
But walk with clearer eyes and ears this path that wandereth,
And see undrugged in evening light the decent inn of death;
For there is good news yet to hear and fine things to be seen,
Before we go to Paradise by way of Kensal Green.

> Gilbert Keith Chesterton had a go at most kinds of writing: plays, novels, short
> stories (he was the creator of Father Brown), criticism, biography, essays,
> journalism – and poems. He never did anything better than this piece of high
> jinks. Non-Londoners may need to be told that Kensal Green is a large cemetery
> off the Harrow Road.

To Be a Pilgrim

JOHN BUNYAN

He who would valiant be
  'Gainst all disaster,
Let him in constancy
  Follow the Master.
There's no discouragement
Shall make him once relent
His first avowed intent
  To be a pilgrim.

Whoso beset him round
  With dismal stories,
Do but themselves confound –
  His strength the more is.
No foes shall stay his might,
Though he with giants fight:
He will make good his right
  To be a pilgrim.

Since, Lord, thou dost defend
  Us with Thy Spirit,
We know we at the end
  Shall life inherit.
Then fancies flee away!
I'll fear not what men say,
I'll labour night and day
  To be a pilgrim.

Bunyan's great religious allegory Pilgrim's Progress was, for generations, to be found alongside the Bible in almost every literate household in the land. He was a Roundhead soldier and a Baptist minister, so puritanical that he banned singing in his church – an irony in view of the later popularity of this hymn.

210   # The Old Familiar Faces

CHARLES LAMB

I have had playmates, I have had companions,
In my days of childhood, in my joyful school-days,
All, all are gone, the old familiar faces.

I have been laughing, I have been carousing,
Drinking late, sitting late, with my bosom cronies,
All, all are gone, the old familiar faces.

I loved a love once, fairest among women:
Closed are her doors on me, I must not see her –
All, all are gone, the old familiar faces.

I have a friend, a kinder friend has no man;
Like an ingrate, I left my friend abruptly;
Left him, to muse on the old familiar faces.

Ghost-like I paced round the haunts of my childhood,
Earth seemed a desert I was bound to traverse,
Seeking to find the old familiar faces.

Friend of my bosom, thou more than a brother,
Why wert thou not born in my father's dwelling?
So might we talk of the old familiar faces.

How some they have died, and some they have left me,
And some are taken from me; all are departed;
All, all are gone, the old familiar faces.

Lamb is remembered chiefly for his whimsical Essays of Elia but he also
wrote poems and works for children. If this poem is sentimental it also captures
memorably a thought or mood that must have come to most people at some
time in their lives. It is perhaps interesting that he wrote it when still in his
early twenties.

That Time of Year Thou Mayst in Me Behold

WILLIAM SHAKESPEARE

That time of year thou mayst in me behold
When yellow leaves, or none, or few, do hang
Upon those boughs which shake against the cold,
Bare ruin'd choirs, where late the sweet birds sang.
In me thou see'st the twilight of such day
As after sunset fadeth in the west,
Which, by and by, black night doth take away,
Death's second self, that seals up all in rest.
In me thou see'st the glowing of such fire,
That on the ashes of his youth doth lie,
As the death-bed whereon it must expire,
Consum'd with that which it was nourish'd by.
    This thou perceiv'st which makes thy love more strong,
    To love that well which thou must leave ere long.

Of all English poets Shakespeare excelled at packing a great deal of meaning
into a few words, but even he never produced anything more concentrated than
the picture of autumn in the first four lines here, especially the phrase 'bare
ruined choirs'. The choir is the part of a church where the choristers sing, a
comparison with the boughs occupied by the singing birds.

For the Fallen

LAURENCE BINYON

With proud thanksgiving, a mother for her children,
England mourns for her dead across the sea.
Flesh of her flesh they were, spirit of her spirit,
Fallen in the cause of the free.

Solemn the drums thrill: Death august and royal
Sings sorrow up into immortal spheres.
There is music in the midst of desolation
And a glory that shines upon our tears.

They went with songs to the battle, they were young,
Straight of limb, true of eye, steady and aglow.
They were staunch to the end against odds uncounted,
They fell with their faces to the foe.

They shall grow not old, as we that are left grow old:
Age shall not weary them, nor the years condemn.
At the going down of the sun and in the morning
We will remember them.

They mingle not with their laughing comrades again;
They sit no more at familiar tables of home;
They have no lot in our labour of the day-time;
They sleep beyond England's foam.

But where our desires are and our hopes profound,
Felt as a well-spring that is hidden from sight,
To the innermost heart of their own land they are known
As the stars are known to the Night;

As the stars that shall be bright when we are dust,
Moving in marches upon the heavenly plain,
As the stars that are starry in the time of our darkness,
To the end, to the end, they remain.

Every year this poem is brought back to the mind at the approach of Armistice
Day. Its measured tone may give it the appearance of a commentary after the
event; in fact Binyon wrote it within the first few weeks of war. Like Kipling at
the same stage, he sensed that a great national effort was about to be required.

Auguries of Innocence 213

WILLIAM BLAKE

To see a World in a Grain of Sand
And a Heaven in a Wild Flower,
Hold Infinity in the palm of your hand
And Eternity in an hour.

A Robin Red breast in a Cage
Puts all Heaven in a Rage.
A dove house fill'd with doves & Pigeons
Shudders Hell thro' all its regions.
A dog starv'd at his Master's Gate
Predicts the ruin of the State.
A Horse misus'd upon the Road
Calls to Heaven for Human blood.
Each outcry of the hunted Hare
A fibre from the Brain does tear.
A Skylark wounded in the wing
A Cherubim does cease to sing.
The Game Cock clip'd & arm'd for fight
Does the Rising Sun affright.
Every Wolf's & Lion's howl
Raises from Hell a Human Soul.
The wild deer, wand'ring here & there,
Keeps the Human Soul from Care.
The Lamb misus'd breeds Public strife
And yet forgives the Butcher's Knife.
The Bat that flits at close of Eve
Has left the Brain that won't Believe.
The Owl that calls upon the Night
Speaks the Unbeliever's fright.
He who shall hurt the little Wren
Shall never be belov'd by Men.
He who the Ox to wrath has mov'd
Shall never be by Woman lov'd.
The wanton Boy that kills the Fly
Shall feel the Spider's enmity.
He who torments the Chafer's sprite
Weaves a Bower in endless Night.
The Catterpiller on the Leaf
Repeats to thee thy Mother's grief.
Kill not the Moth nor Butterfly,
For the Last Judgment draweth nigh.

. . . .

[continued]

A truth that's told with bad intent
Beats all the Lies you can invent.

. . . .

He who mocks the Infant's Faith
Shall be mock'd in Age & Death.
He who shall teach the Child to Doubt
The rotting Grave shall ne'er get out.
He who respects the Infant's faith
Triumphs over Hell & Death.

. . . .

He who replies to words of Doubt
Doth put the Light of Knowledge out.
The Strongest Poison ever known
Came from Caesar's Laurel Crown.

. . . .

He who Doubts from what he sees
Will ne'er Believe, do what you Please.
If the Sun & Moon should doubt,
They'd immediately Go out.
To be in a Passion you Good may do,
But no Good if a Passion is in you.
The Whore & Gambler, by the State
Licenc'd, build that Nation's Fate.
The Harlot's cry from Street to Street
Shall weave Old England's winding Sheet.
The Winner's Shout, the Loser's Curse,
Dance before dead England's Hearse.
Every Night & every Morn
Some to Misery are Born.
Every Morn & every Night
Some are Born to sweet delight.
Some are Born to sweet delight,
Some are Born to Endless Night.
We are led to Believe a Lie
When we see not Thro' the Eye
Which was Born in a Night to perish in a Night
When the Soul Slept in Beams of Light.

God Appears & God is Light
To those poor Souls who dwell in Night,
But does a Human Form Display
To those who dwell in Realms of Day.

Blake's universe is a mysterious place but the general drift of these 'auguries' –
significant remarks or proverbs – seems clear enough with their curiously
modern-sounding insistence on the inviolability of all forms of life. Cockfighting
(lines 17–18) was not finally prohibited by English law until 1849.
The second half of this selection gives us Blake's reflections on faith, doubt,
predestination and various other matters, leading up to a visionary climax
where I for one cannot follow him. He wrote the lines out as parts of a single
poem but seems to have deliberately scrambled the order in which the ideas are
arranged.

Crossing the Bar   214

ALFRED, LORD TENNYSON

Sunset and evening star,
    And one clear call for me!
And may there be no moaning of the bar,
    When I put out to sea,

But such a tide as moving seems asleep,
    Too full for sound and foam,
When that which drew from out the boundless deep
    Turns again home.

Twilight and evening bell,
    And after that the dark!
And may there be no sadness of farewell,
    When I embark;

For tho' from out our bourne of Time and Place
    The flood may bear me far,
I hope to see my Pilot face to face
    When I have crost the bar.

Tennyson wrote this in twenty minutes on the Isle of Wight ferry three years
before his death. On hearing him recite it that evening, his son told him it was
the crown of his life's work. He directed that it should be put at the end of all
editions of his poems. The 'bar' is the sandbank across the harbour mouth.

The Solitary Reaper

215

WILLIAM WORDSWORTH

Behold her, single in the field,
Yon solitary Highland lass!
Reaping and singing by herself:
Stop here, or gently pass!
Alone she cuts and binds the grain,
And sings a melancholy strain;
O listen! for the vale profound
Is overflowing with the sound.

No nightingale did ever chaunt
More welcome notes to weary bands
Of travellers in some shady haunt,
Among Arabian sands;
A voice so thrilling ne'er was heard
In spring-time from the cuckoo-bird,
Breaking the silence of the seas
Among the farthest Hebrides.

Will no one tell me what she sings?
Perhaps the plaintive numbers flow
For old, unhappy, far-off things,
And battles long ago;
Or is it some more humble lay,
Familiar matter of today?
Some natural sorrow, loss, or pain
That has been, and may be again?

Whate'er the theme, the maiden sang
As if her song could have no ending;
I saw her singing at her work,
And o'er the sickle bending;
I listened, motionless and still;
And, as I mounted up the hill,
The music in my heart I bore
Long after it was heard no more.

Of all our poets of the countryside, Wordsworth is the one who most gives the sense of knowing the subject intimately, the places and the people alike. Here for once he seems detached – but only because of a language difficulty. He could not make out the meaning of the lass's song because she was singing in Scottish Gaelic.

On His Mistress, the Queen of Bohemia 216

SIR HENRY WOTTON

You meaner beauties of the night,
    That poorly satisfy our eyes
More by your number than your light,
    You common people of the skies;
    What are you when the moon shall rise?

You curious chanters of the wood,
    That warble forth Dame Nature's lays,
Thinking your passions understood
    By your weak accents; what's your praise
    When Philomel her voice shall raise?

You violets that first appear,
    By your pure purple mantles known
Like the proud virgins of the year,
    As if the spring were all your own;
    What are you when the rose is blown?

So, when my mistress shall be seen
    In form and beauty of her mind,
By virtue first, then choice, a Queen,
    Tell me, if she were not designed
    The eclipse and glory of her kind.

Wotton was a diplomat, for many years English representative in Venice, then a powerful independent republic. In 1620 he went on a special mission to Vienna on behalf of Elizabeth of Bohemia, who was our King James's daughter. The lady seems to have been Wotton's mistress only in the sense that he was her servant.

217 You Are Old, Father William

LEWIS CARROLL

'You are old, Father William,' the young man said,
    'And your hair has become very white;
And yet you incessently stand on your head –
    Do you think, at your age, it is right?'

'In my youth,' Father William replied to his son,
    'I feared it might injure the brain;
But, now that I'm perfectly sure I have none,
    Why, I do it again and again.'

'You are old,' said the youth, 'As I mentioned before,
    And have grown most uncommonly fat;
Yet you turned a back-somersault in at the door –
    Pray, what is the reason of that?'

'In my youth,' said the sage, as he shook his grey locks,
    'I kept all my limbs very supple
By the use of this ointment – one shilling the box –
    Allow me to sell you a couple?'

'You are old,' said the youth, 'and your jaws are too weak
    For anything tougher than suet;
Yet you finished the goose, with the bones and the beak –
    Pray, how did you manage to do it?'

'In my youth,' said his father, 'I took to the law,
    And argued each case with my wife;
And the muscular strength, which it gave to my jaw,
    Has lasted the rest of my life.'

'You are old,' said the youth, 'one would hardly suppose
    That your eye was as steady as ever;
Yet you balanced an eel on the end of your nose –
    What made you so awfully clever?'

'I have answered three questions, and that is enough,'
    Said his father. 'Don't give yourself airs!
Do you think I can listen all day to such stuff?
    Be off, or I'll kick you downstairs!'

This poem, from Alice in Wonderland, has been enjoyed by generations as a sheer comic fantasy. It is actually a parody of a pious, improving piece by Southey called 'The Old Man's Comforts and How He Gained Them'. Lewis Carroll's original readers would have known that and no doubt got a guilty thrill out of the mockery.

November Sky

EDWARD THOMAS

November's days are thirty.
November's earth is dirty,
Those thirty days, from first to last;
And the prettiest things on ground are the paths
With morning and evening hobnails dinted,
With foot and wing-tip overprinted
Or separately charactered,
Of little beast and little bird.
The fields are mashed by sheep, the roads
Make the worst going, the best the woods
Where dead leaves upward and downward scatter.
Few care for the mixture of earth and water,
Twig, leaf, flint, thorn,
Straw, feather, all that men scorn,
Pounded up and sodden by flood,
Condemned as mud.

But of all the months when earth is greener
Not one has clean skies that are cleaner.
Clean and clear and sweet and cold,
They shine above the earth so old,
While the after-tempest cloud
Sails over in silence though winds are loud,
Till the full moon in the east
Looks at the planet in the west
And earth is silent as it is black,
Yet not unhappy for its lack.
Up from the dirty earth men stare:
One imagines a refuge there
Above the mud, in the pure bright
Of the cloudless heavenly light:
Another loves earth and November more dearly
Because without them, he sees clearly,
The sky would be nothing more to his eye
Than he, in any case, is to the sky;
He loves even the mud whose dyes
Renounce all brightness to the skies.

*The detail in Thomas's poems is so closely seen and felt that it is easy to
imagine he wrote on the spot, actually standing in the field or wood he was
describing. At the same time he manages here to convey the general picture of
the whole of the countryside under the November sky with its characteristic
lighting effects.*

219

Say Not the Struggle Nought Availeth

ARTHUR HUGH CLOUGH

Say not the struggle nought availeth,
The labour and the wounds are vain,
The enemy faints not, nor faileth,
And as things have been, things remain.

If hopes were dupes, fears may be liars;
It may be, in yon smoke concealed,
Your comrades chase e'en now the fliers,
And, but for you, possess the field.

For while the tired waves, vainly breaking,
Seem here no painful inch to gain,
Far back through creeks and inlets making
Came, silent, flooding in, the main.

And not by eastern windows only,
When daylight comes, comes in the light,
In front the sun climbs slow, how slowly,
But westward, look, the land is bright.

*In this best known of his poems Clough was not writing of a real physical battle
but of his own spiritual struggles: the wounds and the enemy are not to be
taken literally. But as if by accident it does read like a call to arms, and Sir
Winston Churchill made a great impact by quoting part of it in a broadcast to
the nation in 1941.*

To Be, or Not to Be

WILLIAM SHAKESPEARE

To be, or not to be: that is the question:
Whether 'tis nobler in the mind to suffer
The slings and arrows of outrageous fortune,
Or to take arms against a sea of troubles,
And by opposing end them? To die: to sleep;
No more; and, by a sleep to say we end
The heart-ache and the thousand natural shocks
That flesh is heir to, 'tis a consummation
Devoutly to be wish'd. To die, to sleep;
To sleep; perchance to dream: ay, there's the rub;
For in that sleep of death what dreams may come
When we have shuffled off this mortal coil,
Must give us pause. There's the respect
That makes calamity of so long life;
For who would bear the whips and scorns of time,
The oppressor's wrong, the proud man's contumely,
The pangs of dispriz'd love, the law's delay,
The insolence of office, and the spurns
That patient merit of the unworthy takes,
When he himself might his quietus make
With a bare bodkin? Who would fardels bear,
To grunt and sweat under a weary life,
But that the dread of something after death,
The undiscover'd country from whose bourn
No traveller returns, puzzles the will,
And makes us rather bear those ills we have,
Than fly to others that we know not of?
Thus conscience does make cowards of us all;
And thus the native hue of resolution
Is sicklied o'er with the pale cast of thought,
And enterprises of great pith and moment
With this regard their currents turn awry,
And lose the name of action.

This soliloquy of Hamlet's in the third act of the play must be the most famous
dramatic speech in the world and at one time all sorts of people could recite it or
parts of it. But even those familiar with it may find out more from an attentive
reading than they thought was there, especially in the latter part. Fardels are
bundles or baggage.

221 # Ye Mariners of England

THOMAS CAMPBELL

Ye Mariners of England
That guard our native seas!
Whose flag has braved, a thousand years,
The battle and the breeze!
Your glorious standard launch again
To match another foe;
And sweep through the deep,
While the stormy winds do blow!
While the battle rages loud and long
And the stormy winds do blow.

The spirits of your fathers
Shall start from every wave –
For the deck it was their field of fame,
And Ocean was their grave:
Where Blake and mighty Nelson fell
Your manly hearts shall glow,
As ye sweep through the deep,
While the stormy winds do blow!
While the battle rages loud and long
And the stormy winds do blow.

Britannia needs no bulwarks,
No towers along the steep;
Her march is o'er the mountain-waves,
Her home is on the deep.
With thunders from her native oak
She quells the floods below,
As they roar on the shore,
When the stormy winds do blow!
When the battle rages loud and long,
And the stormy winds do blow.

The meteor flag of England
Shall yet terrific burn;
Till danger's troubled night depart
And the star of peace return.
Then, then, ye ocean-warriors!

Our song and feast shall flow
To the fame of your name,
When the storm has ceased to blow!
When the fiery fight is heard no more,
And the storm has ceased to blow.

Campbell was a Scot but he made no bones about referring to our whole nation as England, aware perhaps that 'ye mariners of Britain' was not much of a phrase – Britannia of course was a different matter. This resounding battle-hymn was written in the 1800s, when England, or Britain, needed a powerful fleet as never before.

Young and Old   222

CHARLES KINGSLEY

When all the world is young, lad,
    And all the trees are green;
And every goose a swan, lad,
    And every lass a queen;
Then hey for boot and horse, lad,
    And round the world away;
Young blood must have its course, lad,
    And every dog his day.

When all the world is old, lad,
    And all the trees are brown;
And all the sport is stale, lad,
    And all the wheels run down;
Creep home, and take your place there,
    The spent and maimed among;
God grant you find one face there,
    You loved when all was young.

Kingsley was a prolific and popular author who wrote, among other things, what used to be one of the most famous of all children's books, The Water Babies. This characteristic song is included in it. The thought or message is not strikingly original but it is expressed very directly and aptly and in a memorable form.

223   I Remember, I Remember

THOMAS HOOD

I remember, I remember,
The house where I was born,
The little window where the sun
Came peeping in at morn;
He never came a wink too soon,
Nor brought too long a day,
But now, I often wish the night
Had borne my breath away!

I remember, I remember,
The roses, red and white,
The violets, and the lily-cups,
Those flowers made of light!
The lilacs where the robin built,
And where my brother set
The laburnum on his birthday, –
The tree is living yet!

I remember, I remember,
Where I was used to swing,
And thought the air must rush as fresh
To swallows on the wing;
My spirit flew in feathers then,
That is so heavy now,
And summer pools could hardly cool
The fever on my brow!

I remember, I remember,
The fir trees dark and high;
I used to think their slender tops
Were close against the sky:
It was a childish ignorance,
But now 'tis little joy
To know I'm farther off from heaven
Than when I was a boy.

This is one of those poems which people often recognise – the first few lines at least – without being able to name the author. Some may find it sentimental; nevertheless it does conjure up quite vividly the dejected mood in which we recall our childhood and fancy for a time that it was better than the present.

Old Meg

JOHN KEATS

Old Meg she was a gipsy,
    And lived upon the moors,
Her bed it was the brown heath turf,
    And her house was out of doors.

Her apples were swart blackberries,
    Her currants pods o' broom,
Her wine was dew of the wild white rose,
    Her book a churchyard tomb.

Her brothers were the craggy hills,
    Her sisters larchen trees –
Alone with her great family
    She lived as she did please.

No breakfast had she many a morn,
    No dinner many a noon,
And 'stead of supper she would stare
    Full hard against the moon.

But every morn of woodbine fresh
    She made her garlanding,
And every night the dark glen yew
    She wove, and she would sing.

And with her fingers old and brown
    She plaited mats o'rushes,
And gave them to the cottagers
    She met among the bushes.

Old Meg was brave as Margaret Queen
    And tall as Amazon.
An old red blanket cloak she wore,
    A chip hat had she on.
God rest her aged bones somewhere –
    She died full long agone!

Meg is a character in Walter Scott's novel Guy Mannering. She appealed
greatly to Keats, who is supposed to have 'scribbled' this ballad in a letter to his
young sister while travelling to Scotland. Scott's work helped to start the vogue
for all things Scottish that swept England and elsewhere at this time.

225

Scots, Wha Hae

ROBERT BURNS

Scots, wha hae wi' Wallace bled,
Scots, wham Bruce has aften led,
Welcome to your gory bed,
　　Or to victory!

Now's the day, and now's the hour;
See the front o' battle lour,
See approach proud Edward's power –
　　Chains and slaverie!

Wha will be a traitor knave?
Wha can fill a coward's grave?
Wha sae base as be a slave? –
　　Let him turn, and flee!

Wha for Scotland's King and Law
Freedom's sword will strongly draw,
Freeman stand or freeman fa',
　　Let him follow me!

By Oppression's woes and pains,
By your sons in servile chains,
We will drain our dearest veins,
　　But they shall be free!

Lay the proud usurpers low!
Tyrants fall in every foe!
Liberty's in every blow!
　　Let us do, or die!

*This poem quickly became a kind of unofficial anthem of the Scottish nation
and fittingly commemorates St Andrew's Day. In the way of patriotic pieces it
refers to an ancient triumph, the defeat of the English at Bannockburn in 1314,
but so rousingly that only the hardest Sassenach heart could fail to be touched
by it.*

November 226

HARTLEY COLERIDGE

The mellow year is hasting to its close;
The little birds have almost sung their last,
Their small notes twitter in the dreary blast –
That shrill-piped harbinger of early snows:
The patient beauty of the scentless rose,
Oft with the Morn's hoar crystal quaintly glassed,
Hangs, a pale mourner for the summer past,
And makes a little summer where it grows:
In the chill sunshine of the faint brief day
The dusky waters shudder as they shine,
The russet leaves obstruct the straggling way
Of oozy brooks, which no deep banks define,
And the gaunt woods, in ragged, scant array,
Wrap their old limbs with sombre ivy twine.

Hartley was the eldest son of Samuel Taylor Coleridge, like his father a poet,
but one who never achieved any real distinction except in his sonnets. This
example shows him at his best with its fine passage on the late wild rose and
the very closely observed and carefully described picture of autumn sun on
water.

Little Billee

WILLIAM MAKEPEACE THACKERAY

There were three sailors in Bristol City,
Who took a boat and went to sea.

But first with beef and captain's biscuit,
And pickled pork they loaded she.

There was guzzling Jack and gorging Jimmy,
And the youngest he was little Bil-ly.

Now very soon they were so greedy,
They didn't leave not one spilt pea.

Says guzzling Jack to gorging Jimmy
I am confounded hung-ery.

Says gorging Jim to guzzling Jacky,
We have no wittles, so we must eat we.

Says guzzling Jack to gorging Jimmy,
O gorging Jim, what a fool you be.

There's little Bill as is young and tender,
We're old and tough – so let's eat he.

O Bill, we're going to kill and eat you,
So undo the collar of your chemie.

When Bill he heard this information,
He used his pocket-handkerchee.

O let me say my Catechism,
As my poor mammy taught to me.

Make haste, make haste, says guzzling Jacky,
Whilst Jim pulled out his snicker-snee.

So Bill went up the main top-gallant mast,
When down he fell on his bended knee.

He scarce had said his Catechism,
When up he jumps: 'There's land I see!

'There's Jerusalem and Madagascar,
And North and South Ameri-key.

'There's the British fleet a-riding at anchor,
With Admiral Napier, K.C.B.'

So when they came to the Admiral's vessel,
He hanged fat Jack and flogged Jim-my.

But as for little Bill, he made him
The Captain of a Seventy-three.

Thackeray's reputation rests on Vanity Fair *and other novels, but he contributed to* Punch *and wrote a good deal of verse, some of it in the form of comic ballads. This one is partly a take-off of the tales of adventure at sea that were current at that time and partly a piece of sheer fantasy for the fun of it.*

She Walks in Beauty 228

GEORGE GORDON, LORD BYRON

She walks in beauty, like the night
    Of cloudless climes and starry skies;
And all that's best of dark and bright
    Meet in her aspect and her eyes:
Thus mellow'd to that tender light
    Which heaven to gaudy day denies.

One shade the more, one ray the less,
    Had half impair'd the nameless grace
Which waves in every raven tress,
    Or softly lightens o'er her face;
Where thoughts serenely sweet express
    How pure, how dear their dwelling-place.

And on that cheek, and o'er that brow,
    So soft, so calm, yet eloquent,
The smiles that win, the tints that glow,
    But tell of days in goodness spent,
A mind at peace with all below,
    A heart whose love is innocent!

According to the dictionaries, a lyric nowadays is nothing more or less than a poem that briefly expresses the writer's personal thoughts and feelings. But by origin a lyric has connections with songs and singing, and this famous one of Byron's certainly seems to call for setting to music, as has of course been done.

229

The Tables Turned:
An Evening Scene

WILLIAM WORDSWORTH

Up! up! my friend, and quit your books;
Or surely you'll grow double.
Up! up! my friend, and clear your looks,
Why all this toil and trouble?

The sun above the mountain's head,
A freshening lustre mellow,
Through all the long green fields has spread,
His first sweet evening yellow.

Books! 'tis a dull and endless strife,
Come, hear the woodland linnet,
How sweet his music; on my life
There's more of wisdom in it.

And hark! how blithe the throstle sings!
He, too, is no mean preacher;
Come forth into the light of things,
Let nature be your teacher.

She has a world of ready wealth,
Our minds and hearts to bless –
Spontaneous wisdom breathed by health,
Truth breathed by cheerfulness.

One impulse from a vernal wood
May teach you more of man;
Of moral evil and of good,
Than all the sages can.

Sweet is the lore which nature brings;
Our meddling intellect
Misshapes the beauteous forms of things; –
We murder to dissect.

Enough of science and of art;
Close up those barren leaves;
Come forth, and bring with you a heart
That watches and receives.

*Wordsworth was far too civilised a man to believe that science and art were not
important, but he did believe very strongly, and was one of the first to say, that
contact with nature was even more important. He is not just telling his friend to
get out in the open air, he means literally that mountains and woods have
lessons to teach.*

The Soldier   230

RUPERT BROOKE

If I should die, think only this of me;
    That there's some corner of a foreign field
That is for ever England. There shall be
    In that rich earth a richer dust concealed;
A dust whom England bore, shaped, made aware,
    Gave, once, her flowers to love, her ways to roam,
A body of England's breathing English air,
    Washed by the rivers, blest by suns of home.

And think, this heart, all evil shed away,
    A pulse in the eternal mind, no less
        Gives somewhere back the thoughts by England given;
Her sights and sounds; dreams happy as her day;
    And laughter, learnt of friends and gentleness,
        In hearts at peace, under an English heaven.

*Brooke died not on the Western Front as was once often believed, but of blood
poisoning on his way to fight in the Dardanelles campaign. He died on a
hospital ship and was buried on the Greek island of Scyros. Only a couple of
years later it had become impossible to write in the vein of this famous sonnet,
but that does not affect it, and anyway its subject is not war but England.*

231 Heaven's Last Best Work

ALEXANDER POPE

Oh! blest with temper, whose unclouded ray
Can make to-morrow cheerful as to-day;
She, who can love a Sister's charms, or hear
Sighs for a Daughter with unwounded ear;
She, who ne'er answers till a Husband cools,
Or, if she rules him, never shows she rules;
Charms by accepting, by submitting sways,
Yet has her humour most, when she obeys;
Let Fops or Fortune fly which way they will,
Disdains all loss of Tickets, or Codille;
Spleen, Vapours, or Small-Pox, above them all,
And Mistress of herself, tho' China fall.
    And yet, believe me, good as well as ill,
Woman's at best a Contradiction still.
Heav'n when it strives to polish all it can
Its last best work, but forms a softer Man:
Picks from each sex, to make the Fav'rite blest,
Your love of Pleasure, our desire of Rest;
Blends, in exception to all gen'ral rules,
Your taste of Follies, with our Scorn of Fools,
Reserve with Frankness, Art with Truth ally'd,
Courage with Softness, Modesty with Pride,
Fix'd Principles, with Fancy ever new;
Shakes all together, and produces – You.

*In his satirical poems Pope could be viciously cruel and he was not an amiable
sort, but in this extract from his so-called moral essay Of the Characters of
Women he shows great sympathy and fondness, even if present-day feminists
would not care for some of what he says. Temper is calmness, codille, call at
cards and china, porcelain.*

A Song of the GPO

GERRY HAMILL

I'm the bloke that's trained to sit behind the public stamp machines
When you come to post a letter in the rain.
    'Ow I laugh to 'ear the curses
    As they fiddle in their purses
For a 10p piece that won't pop out again.

It's me job to put the rolls of stamps behind the little slot
So you get one when you pokes your money through.
    'Ow I giggle at the slangin'
    And the nasty-tempered bangin'
If it don't come out when it's supposed to do.

If the stamp machines get busy I put up me 'empty' signs,
Then I makes the tea and 'as me little snack,
    But the stream of filthy language
    Doesn't put me off me sangwidge
'Cos I'm taught to smile and never answer back.

Now, the proper way to buy a stamp is from the counter clerk,
Who provides a queue where you can 'ang about;
    If you don't know any better
    Than to write yer flippin' letter
After five, then you deserve to go without.

> The golden age of light or comic verse was probably the nineteenth century, but some of it can be still found in weekly magazines. Gerry Hamill's brilliantly-written frolic makes it easier to bear those times when we start believing that there really is a grinning little goblin inside the infuriating machine.

233

Sailing to Byzantium

W. B. YEATS

That is no country for old men. The young
In one another's arms, birds in the trees
– Those dying generations – at their song,
The salmon-falls, the mackerel-crowded seas,
Fish, flesh, or fowl, commend all summer long
Whatever is begotten, born, and dies.
Caught in that sensual music all neglect
Monuments of unageing intellect.

An aged man is but a paltry thing,
A tattered coat upon a stick, unless
Soul chap its hands and sing, and louder sing
For every tatter in its mortal dress,
Nor is there singing school but studying
Monuments of its own magnificence;
And therefore I have sailed the seas and come
To the holy city of Byzantium.

O sages standing in God's holy fire
As in the gold mosaic of a wall,
Come from the holy fire, perne in a gyre,
And be the singing-masters of my soul.
Consume my heart away; sick with desire
And fastened to a dying animal
It knows not what it is; and gather me
Into the artifice of eternity.

Once out of nature I shall never take
My bodily form from any natural thing,
But such a form as Grecian goldsmiths make
Of hammered gold and gold enamelling
To keep a drowsy Emperor awake;
Or set upon a golden bough to sing
To lords and ladies of Byzantium
Of what is past, or passing, or to come.

Many of Yeats's later poems, like this one, are based on a private system of
mythology and the occult. So Byzantium is not the historical city (later
Constantinople, now Istanbul) but some sort of symbol of ideal art. In general
the meaning is far from clear, but the colour and the sense of excitement do
communicate themselves.

Peter Grimes

GEORGE CRABBE

Thus by himself compelled to live each day,
To wait for certain hours the tide's delay;
At the same times the same dull views to see,
The bounding marsh-bank and the blighted tree;
The water only, when the tides were high,
When low, the mud half-covered and half-dry;
The sun-burnt tar that blisters on the planks,
And bank-side stakes in their uneven ranks;
Heaps of entangled weeds that slowly float,
As the tide rolls by the impeded-boat.
　　When tides were neap, and, in the sultry day,
Through the tall bounding mud-banks made their way,
Which on each side rose swelling, and below
The dark warm flood ran silently and slow;
There anchoring, Peter chose from man to hide,
There hang his head, and view the lazy tide
In its hot slimy channel slowly glide;
Where the small eels that left the deeper way
For the warm shore, within the shallows play;
Where gaping mussels, left upon the mud,
Slope their slow passage to the fallen flood; –
Here dull and hopeless he'd lie down and trace
How sidelong crabs had scrawled their crooked race;
Or sadly listen to the tuneless cry
Of fishing gull or clanging golden-eye;
What time the sea birds to the marsh would come,
And the loud bittern, from the bull-rush home,
Gave from the salt-ditch side the bellowing boom;
He nursed the feelings these dull scenes produce,
And loved to stop beside the opening sluice;
Where the small stream, confined in narrow bound,
Ran with a dull, unvaried, saddening sound;
Where all, presented to the eye or ear,
Oppressed the soul with misery, grief, and fear.

Crabbe portrays the Suffolk countryside and its people in all their aspects, not
least the sadder and grimmer ones. This extract from his long poem, The
Borough, shows the boredom and emptiness of solitude. The opera Peter
Grimes by Benjamin Britten is based on this poem.

235 # La Figlia Che Piange

O quam te memorem virgo . . .

T. S. ELIOT

Stand on the highest pavement of the stair –
Lean on a garden urn –
Weave, weave the sunlight in your hair –
Clasp your flowers to you with a pained surprise –
Fling them to the ground and turn
With a fugitive resentment in your eyes:
But weave, weave the sunlight in your hair.

So I would have had him leave,
So I would have had her stand and grieve,
So he would have left
As the soul leaves the body torn and bruised,
As the mind deserts the body it has used.
I should find
Some way incomparably light and deft,
Some way we both should understand,
Simple and faithless as a smile and shake of the hand.

She turned away, but with the autumn weather
Compelled my imagination many days,
Many days and many hours:
Her hair over her arms and her arms full of flowers.
And I wonder how they should have been together!
I should have lost a gesture and a pose.
Sometimes these cogitations still amaze
The troubled midnight and the moon's repose.

The title means 'the weeping girl'. This is one of Eliot's comparatively
straightforward poems. The 'he' character is presumably some other admirer of
the girl's, more brutal than the Eliot character, who seems not much nicer by
the end. But the picture of the girl on the stair is clear, vivid and memorable.

Echo

CHRISTINA ROSSETTI

Come to me in the silence of the night;
   Come in the speaking silence of a dream;
Come with soft rounded cheeks and eyes as bright
     As sunlight on a stream;
       Come back in tears,
O memory, hope, love of finished years.

O dream how sweet, too sweet, too bitter sweet,
   Whose wakening should have been in Paradise,
Where souls brimfull of love abide and meet;
     Where thirsting longing eyes
       Watch the slow door
That opening, letting in, lets out no more.

Yet come to me in dreams, that I may live
   My very life again though cold in death:
Come back to me in dreams, that I may give
     Pulse for pulse, breath for breath:
       Speak low, lean low,
As long ago, my love, how long ago!

*Of all Christina's large output of short passionate lyrics this is one of the most
popular and striking. Her devoted brother W. M. Rossetti, who edited her
works, noted that this was written in December 1854, when she was just
twenty-four, so 'finished years' and 'long ago' can hardly be true. But the
feeling is true.*

237

The First Nowell

ANONYMOUS

The first Nowell the angel did say
Was to certain poor shepherds in fields as they lay;
In fields where they lay keeping their sheep,
On a cold winter's night that was so deep.

Nowell, Nowell, Nowell, Nowell,
Born is the King of Israel.

They looked up and saw a star,
Shining in the east, beyond them far,
And to the earth it gave great light,
And so it continued both day and night.

Chorus.

And by the light of that same star,
Three Wise Man came from country far;
To seek for a King was their intent,
And to follow the star wherever it went.

Chorus.

This star drew nigh to the north-west,
O'er Bethlehem it took its rest,
And there it did both stop and stay,
Right over the place where Jesus lay.

Chorus.

Then entered in those Wise Men three,
Full reverently upon their knee,
And offered there, in His presence,
Their gold, and myrrh, and frankincense.

Chorus.

Then let us all with one accord,
Sing praises to our Heavenly Lord,
That hath made heav'n and earth of nought,
And with his blood mankind hath bought.

Chorus.

We now offer a selection of carols, beginning with what is perhaps the most
famous of all. The tune is traditional. The word Nowell or Noel goes back to
the fourteenth century and at one time is supposed to have been shouted or sung
on its own as an expression of joy to commemorate the birth of Christ; the word
is connected with 'natal'.

Once in Royal David's City 238

CECIL FRANCES ALEXANDER

Once in royal David's city
 Stood a lowly cattle shed,
Where a mother laid her baby
 In a manger for his bed;
Mary was that mother mild,
Jesus Christ her little child.

He came down to earth from heaven
 Who is God and Lord of all,
And his shelter was a stable,
 And his cradle was a stall;
With the poor and mean and lowly
Lived on earth our Saviour holy.

And through all his wondrous childhood
 He would honour and obey,
Love and watch the lowly maiden,
 In whose gentle arms he lay:
Christian children all must be
Mild, obedient, good as he.

. . . .

And our eyes at last shall see him,
 Through his own redeeming love,
For that Child so dear and gentle
 Is our Lord in heaven above;
And he leads his children on
To the place where he is gone.

Not in that poor lowly stable,
 With the oxen standing by,
We shall see him; but in heaven,
 Set at God's right hand on high;
When like stars his children crowned
All in white shall wait around.

*In this children's hymn Mrs Alexander (author of 'All Things Bright and
Beautiful') commemorates the amazing idea that lies at the heart of the
Christian religion: that God, the almighty creator of Heaven and Earth, should
have come to our world as a poor human child to lead a human life.*

239 # *While Shepherds Watch'd*

NAHUM TATE

While shepherds watch'd their flocks by night,
All seated on the ground,
The Angel of the Lord came down
And glory shone around.

'Fear not,' said he; for mighty dread
Had seized their troubled mind;
'Glad tidings of great joy I bring
To you and all mankind.'

'To you in David's town this day
Is born of David's line
A Saviour, Who is Christ the Lord;
And this shall be the sign:

'The heavenly Babe you there shall find
To human view display'd,
All meanly wrapp'd in swathing bands,
And in a manger laid.'

Thus spake the seraph; and forthwith
Appear'd a shining throng
Of Angels praising God, who thus
Address'd their joyful song:

'All glory be to God on high,
And on the earth be peace;
Good-will henceforth from heaven to men
Begin and never cease.'

The tune of this carol is older than the words and goes back to 1592. Tate was
an Irishman famous for adapting other men's plays, including some of
Shakespeare's. His version of King Lear, with a happy ending, held the stage
for a long time. There was general amazement in 1692 when he was made Poet
Laureate.

Hark! The Herald Angels Sing   240

CHARLES WESLEY

Hark! the herald angels sing
Glory to the new-born king;
Peace on earth and mercy mild,
God and sinners reconciled.
Joyful all ye nations rise,
Join the triumph of the skies;
With the angelic host proclaim,
Christ is born in Bethlehem!

> *Hark! the herald angels sing*
> *Glory to the new-born King.*

Christ, by highest heaven adored,
Christ, the everlasting Lord,
Late in time behold him come,
Offspring of a Virgin's womb,
Veiled in flesh the Godhead see!
Hail the incarnate Deity!
Pleased as man with man to dwell,
Jesus, our Emmanuel.

> *Hark! the herald angels sing*
> *Glory to the new-born King.*

Hail the heaven-born Prince of peace!
Hail the Sun of Righteousness,
Light and life to all he brings,
Risen with healing in his wings.
Mild he lays his glory by,
Born that man no more may die,
Born to raise the sons of earth,
Born to give them second birth.

> *Hark! the herald angels sing*
> *Glory to the new-born King.*

In his book of carols Edward Heath rightly complains that this fine one is often carelessly sung. He comments 'Mendelssohn wrote a stately tune, full of dignity and splendour. We need to sing it at a steady pace with rounded tone, otherwise it becomes trivial.' Wesley, with his brother John, the founder of Methodism, wrote many hymns.

Good King Wenceslas

241

JOHN MASON NEALE

Good King Wenceslas looked out,
    On the Feast of Stephen,
When the snow lay round about,
    Deep, and crisp, and even:
Brightly shone the moon that night,
    Though the frost was cruel,
When a poor man came in sight,
    Gath'ring winter fuel.

'Hither, page, and stand by me,
    If thou know'st it, telling,
Yonder peasant, who is he?
    Where and what his dwelling?'
'Sire, he lives a good league hence,
    Underneath the mountain,
Right against the forest fence,
    By Saint Agnes' fountain.'

'Bring me flesh, and bring me wine,
    Bring me pine-logs hither;
Thou and I will see him dine,
    When we bear them hither.'
Page and monarch, forth they went,
    Forth they went together;
Through the rude wind's wild lament,
    And the bitter weather.

'Sire, the night is darker now,
    And the wind blows stronger;
Fails my heart, I know not how;
    I can go no longer.'
'Mark my footsteps, good my page;
    Tread thou in them boldly:
Thou shalt find in the winter's rage
    Freeze thy blood less coldly.'

In his master's steps he trod,
 Where the snow lay dinted;
Heat was in the very sod
 Which the Saint had printed.
Therefore, Christian men, be sure,
 Wealth or rank possessing,
Ye who now will bless the poor,
 Shall yourselves find blessing.

*John Mason Neale, author of many hymns, wrote these words to fit a sixteenth-
century tune. St Wenceslas was duke of Bohemia (now part of Czechoslovakia)
in the tenth century. He was a godly man who did much to promote
Christianity and after being murdered by his brother was venerated as a martyr,
but the exploit recounted here is imaginary.*

Christmas   242

SIR JOHN BETJEMAN

The bells of waiting Advent ring,
 The Tortoise stove is lit again
And lamp-oil light across the night
 Has caught the streaks of winter rain
In many a stained-glass window sheen.
From Crimson Lake to Hooker's Green.

The holly in the windy hedge
 And round the Manor House the yew
Will soon be stripped to deck the ledge,
 The altar, font and arch and pew,
So that the villagers can say
'The church looks nice' on Christmas Day.

Provincial public houses blaze
 And Corporation tramcars clang,
On lighted tenements I gaze
 Where paper decorations hang,
And bunting in the red Town Hall
Says 'Merry Christmas to you all.'

[continued]

And London shops on Christmas Eve
    Are strung with silver bells and flowers
As hurrying clerks the City leave
    To pigeon-haunted classic towers,
And marbled clouds go scudding by
The many-steepled London sky.

And girls in slacks remember Dad,
    And oafish louts remember Mum,
And sleepless children's hearts are glad,
    And Christmas-morning bells say 'Come!'
Even to shining ones who dwell
Safe in the Dorchester Hotel.

And is it true? And is it true,
    This most tremendous tale of all,
Seen in a stained-glass window's hue,
    A Baby in an ox's stall?
The Maker of the stars and sea
Become a Child on earth for me?

And is it true? For if it is,
    No loving fingers tying strings
Around those tissued fripperies,
    The sweet and silly Christmas things,
Bath salts and inexpensive scent
And hideous tie so kindly meant.

No love that in a family dwells,
    No carolling in a frosty air,
Nor all the steeple-shaking bells
    Can with this single Truth compare –
That God was Man in Palestine
And lives to-day in Bread and Wine.

A splendid poem to express good wishes for Christmas and the New Year.

On the Tombs in Westminster Abbey

FRANCIS BEAUMONT

Mortality, behold and fear,
What a change of flesh is here!
Think how many royal bones
Sleep within this heap of stones,
Hence removed from beds of ease,
Dainty fare, and what might please,
Fretted roofs, and costly shows,
To a roof that flats the nose:
Which proclaims all flesh is grass;
How the world's fair glories pass;
That there is no trust in health,
In youth, in age, in greatness, wealth;
For if such could have reprieved
Those had been immortal lived.
Know from this the world's a snare,
How that greatness is but care,
How all pleasures are but pain,
And how short they do remain:
For here they lie had realms and lands,
That now want strength to stir their hands;
Where from their pulpits sealed with dust
They preach: 'In greatness is no trust'.
Here's an acre sown indeed
With the richest royalest seed

. . . .

Here's a world of pomp and state,
Forgotten, dead, disconsolate;
Think, then, this scythe that mows down kings
Exempts no meaner mortal things.
Then bid the wanton lady tread
Amid these mazes of the dead;
And these truly understood
More shall cool and quench the blood
Than her many sports aday,
And her nightly wanton play.

[continued]

Bid her paint till day of doom,
To this favour she must come.
Bid the merchant gather wealth,
The usurer exact by stealth,
The proud man beat it from his thought,
Yet to this shape all must be brought.

*Beaumont was a leading playwright of his day. In this poem he produces a
powerful variation on the favourite Elizabethan theme of the passing,
temporary nature of royal power, all the more striking then when kings were so
much more elevated above ordinary people than they are now. By a pleasant
irony Beaumont himself was buried in the Abbey.*

244   # To His Coy Mistress

ANDREW MARVELL

Had we but world enough, and time,
This coyness, Lady, were no crime.
We would sit down and think which way
To walk and pass our long love's day.
Thou by the Indian Ganges' side
Should'st rubies find: I by the tide
Of Humber would complain. I would
Love you ten years before the Flood,
And you should, if you please, refuse
Till the conversion of the Jews.
My vegetable love should grow
Vaster then empires, and more slow;
An hundred years should go to praise
Thine eyes and on thy forehead gaze;
Two hundred to adore each breast;
But thirty thousand to the rest;
An age at least to every part,
And the last age should know your heart.
For, Lady, you deserve this state,
Nor would I love at lower rate.

But at my back I always hear
Time's winged chariot hurrying near;
And yonder all before us lie
Deserts of vast eternity.
Thy beauty shall no more be found,
Nor, in thy marble vault, shall sound
My echoing song: then worms shall try
That long preserved virginity,
And your quaint honour turn to dust,
And into ashes all my lust:
The grave's a fine and private place,
But none, I think, do there embrace.

Now therefore, while the youthful hue
Sits on thy skin like morning dew,
And while thy willing soul transpires
At every pore with instant fires,
Now let us sport us while we may,
And now, like amorous birds of prey,
Rather at once our time devour
Than languish in his slow-chapt power.
Let us roll all our strength and all
Our sweetness up into one ball,
And tear our pleasures with rough strife
Through the iron gates of life:
Thus, though we cannot make our sun
Stand still, yet we will make him run.

This poem is one of the flowers of the Metaphysical school of poets who delighted in fanciful and elaborate comparisons. Marvell manages to get real feeling in as well and turns a light-hearted caper into a reflection on love and death. The image near the end is of a cannon-ball smashing through the gates of a fort.

245

Ring Out, *Wild Bells*

ALFRED, LORD TENNYSON

Ring out, wild bells, to the wild sky,
    The flying cloud, the frosty light:
    The year is dying in the night:
Ring out, wild bells, and let him die.

Ring out the old, ring in the new,
    Ring, happy bells, across the snow:
    The year is going, let him go:
Ring out the false, ring in the true.

Ring out the grief that saps the mind,
    For those that here we see no more;
    Ring out the feud of rich and poor,
Ring in redress to all mankind.

Ring out a slowly dying cause,
    And ancient forms of party strife;
    Ring in the nobler modes of life,
With sweeter manners, purer laws.

Ring out the want, the care, the sin,
    The faithless coldness of the times;
    Ring out, ring out my mournful rhymes,
But ring the fuller minstrel in.

Ring out false pride in place and blood,
    The civic slander and the spite;
    Ring in the love of truth and right,
Ring in the common love of good.

Ring out old shapes of foul disease:
    Ring out the narrowing lust of gold;
    Ring out the thousand wars of old,
Ring in the thousand years of peace.

Ring in the valiant man and free,
    The larger heart, the kindlier hand;
    Ring out the darkness of the land,
Ring in the Christ that is to be.

Tennyson's New Year wishes seem to be very much what anybody of goodwill
would wish for the human race, then or now. It is tempting to say that some of
his phrases have a strikingly contemporary ring, but is that a testimony to his
foresight or merely evidence that human problems never change much?
Anyway, let us try to share his optimism.

Acknowledgements

The editor and publisher wish to thank the following for permission to reprint copyright poems. Although every effort has been made to contact the owners of the copyright in poems published in this anthology a few have been impossible to trace. If the owners contact the publisher, correct acknowledgement will be made in future editions.

JOHN ASHBERY
'Fear of Death' from *Selected Poems*, published by Carcanet Press Limited. Reprinted by permission of the publisher.

KENNETH ASHLEY
'Goods Train at Night' from *Up Hill and Down Dale*, published by The Bodley Head. Reproduced by permission of the author.

W. H. AUDEN
'Taller Today' and 'Johnny' from *Collected Poems* and *The English Auden*, published by Faber & Faber. Reprinted by permission of the publisher.

JOHN BETJEMAN
'Sun and Fun,' 'Seaside Golf', 'Slough', 'A Child Ill', 'In Westminster Abbey', 'Christmas', 'The Cottage Hospital' and 'Executive' from *Collected Poems*, published by John Murray Ltd. Reprinted by permission of the publisher.

LAURENCE BINYON
'The Burning of the Leaves' (part of a longer poem); 'For the Fallen'. Reprinted by permission of Mrs Nicolete Gray and the Society of Authors on behalf of the Laurence Binyon Estate.

EDMUND BLUNDEN
'Report on Experience' from *Poems of Many Years*, published by William Collins Sons & Co. Ltd. Reprinted by permission of the Peters Fraser & Dunlop Group.

IDRIS DAVIES
'High Summer on the Mountains', published by Gomer Press. Reprinted by permission of the publisher.

T. S. ELIOT
'The Rum Tum Tugger' and 'La Figlia Che Piange' from *Old Possum's Book of Practical Cats* and *Collected Poems 1909–1962*, published by Faber & Faber. Reprinted by permission of the publisher.

JAMES FENTON
'In a Notebook' from *Memory of War*, published by Penguin Books Ltd. Reprinted by permission of the Peters Fraser & Dunlop Group Ltd.

ROBERT FROST
'Stopping by Woods on a Snowy Evening' from *The Poetry of Robert Frost*, ed. Edward Connery Lathem, published by Jonathan Cape Limited. Reprinted by permission of the publisher and the Estate of Robert Frost.

ROBERT GRAVES
'A Slice of Wedding Cake', '1805', 'One Hard Look', Love Without Hope' and 'Flying Crooked' from *Collected Poems 1975*. 'An English Wood', 'Dead Cow Farm', 'Cold Weather Proverb'. Reprinted by permission of A. P. Watt Limited on behalf of The Executors of the Estate of Robert Graves.

TED HUGHES
'The Howling of Wolves' from *Wodwo*, published by Faber & Faber. Reprinted by permission of the publisher.

ELIZABETH JENNINGS
'The Sparrows' Chorus' and 'The Rabbit's Advice' from *After the Ark*, published by Oxford University Press. Reprinted by permission of David Higham Associates Limited.

LOUIS MACNEICE
'Bagpipe Music' from *The Collected Poems of Louis MacNeice*, published by Faber & Faber. Reprinted by permission of the publisher.

WALTER DE LA MARE
'The Listeners'. Reprinted by permission of the Literary Trustees of Walter de la Mare and the Society of Authors as their representative.

JOHN MASEFIELD
'The West Wind', 'Cargoes', 'To His Mother. C.L.M.'. Reprinted by permission of the Society of Authors as the literary representative of the Estate of John Masefield.

EDWIN MUIR
'The Breaking' from *Collected Poems*, published by Faber & Faber. Reprinted by permission of the publisher.

SYLVIA PLATH
'The Moon and the Yew Tree' from *The Collected Poems of Sylvia Plath*, published by Faber & Faber. Reprinted by permission of Olwyn Hughes.

SIEGFRIED SASSOON
'Attack', 'The General', 'Base Details'. Reprinted by permission of George T. Sassoon.

JAMES STEPHENS
'The Road'. Reprinted by permission of the Society of Authors on behalf of the copyright owner, Mrs Iris Wise.

DYLAN THOMAS
'Light Breaks Where No Sun Shines' from *The Poems*, published by J. M. Dent. Reprinted by permission of David Higham Associates Limited.

R. S. THOMAS
'The Hill Farmer Speaks' and 'The Lonely Farmer' from *An Acre of Land 1952*, published by William Collins Sons & Co. Ltd. Reprinted by permission of Gwydion Thomas.

Index of First Lines

The references are to poem numbers

Index of Authors

The references are to poem numbers